GEORGE FORTY

M4 SHERMAN

GEORGE FORTY

BLANDFORD PRESS
POOLE · NEW YORK · SYDNEY

First published in the UK 1987 by Blandford Press
Link House, West Street, Poole, Dorset BH15 1LL

Distributed in the United States by
Sterling Publishing Co, Inc,
2 Park Avenue, New York, NY 10016

Distributed in Australia by
Capricorn Link (Australia) Pty Ltd
PO Box 665, Lane Cove, NSW 2066

British Library Cataloguing in Publication Data

Forty, George
 The M-4 Sherman. —(Hardware)
 1. Sherman Tank
 I. Title   II. Series
 623.74′752   UG446.5

ISBN 0 7137 1678 9

Series editor: M. G. Burns

Typeset by Keyspools Ltd, Golborne, Lancs
Printed in Great Britain by R. J. Acford, Chichester

**Frontispiece
Thumbing a ride. Men
of the 29th Marines hop
a ride on an obliging
Sherman, while moving
up to take the town of
Ghuta, Okinawa, before
the Japanese can occupy
it (USMC).**

CONTENTS

While I was researching for an earlier book[1] about American tanks in World War Two, I remember receiving an anecdote from one of my correspondents, an American named Frank Woolner, who had served as a reconnaissance tank destroyer Sergeant and later as a combat correspondent with 3rd Armored Division. He wrote that most of the German tankers they captured seemed to have the same stock joke: 'Von off our tanks iss better than ten off yours,' the captured German would say. Then, just about when you had decided to punch the guy on the whiskers, he would shrug, grin and say 'But you always haff eleven!' I would take any odds that the vast majority of those eleven were M4 Shermans of one type or another.

The Sherman was a logical development in the US medium tank line, which began back in the early 1920s and included the M2, M2A1 and M3 in its lineage. It was the most widely used tank of World War Two, appearing in every theatre of operations, and on nearly every battlefield from 1942 onwards. While it was not on a par with the best German tanks, such as the Tiger and Panther, as far as firepower and armoured protection was concerned, its mobility, reliability and general ease of handling made it an excellent tank to fight in. The Sherman was without doubt the most important tank produced during the war by the Western Allies and was built in such staggering quantities as to dwarf all other tank production anywhere in the world. 49,234 Sherman gun tanks of all types were produced by the United States, more than half the entire American wartime tank production and equal to the total combined production of Great Britain and

Sherman burns.
nocked out on the
utskirts of Frankfurt
· a German
anzerfaust team, this
·erman belonging to
h Armored Division,
nird US Army, lives
· to its nickname of the
·onson Lighter'
;eorge F. Hofmann).

Germany. If one adds to that enormous figure all the other variants which used basic M4 components, such as chassis and powerpacks, which included Gun Motor Carriages, Howitzer Motor Carriages and Tracked Recovery Vehicles, then the total is even more mind-boggling.

In common with every other armoured fighting vehicle ever built, the Sherman had its good and bad points. Tank design is always a compromise between the three basic characteristics of firepower, protection and mobility, and when the Sherman was designed in mid-1941, it was considered to be a very good compromise. Events were to prove that it lacked firepower, but its popularity in its original form actually militated against putting this right until far too late in the war to have much effect – apart from the relatively small number of British conversions which mounted the hard hitting 17-pdr anti-tank gun. Firepower was marginally improved with the fitting of the 76 mm gun, but it was left to the Israelis many years later to mount a really effective gun on their Shermans. However, the gun control equipment was excellent and a well-trained Sherman crew could be guaranteed to outshoot most other AFVs, even though their well-aimed rounds might then all bounce off the enemy glacis plate. Protection was disappointing, especially as the German tank guns improved, and it had a penchant for catching fire quickly. Not for nothing did the Germans call it the 'Tommy Cooker', or the Sherman crews themselves refer to it as the 'Ronson Lighter', because it could always be guaranteed to light first time. Yet its straightforward, uncomplicated design, excellent mobility, general ruggedness and ease of maintenance, all added up to an extremely reliable fighting machine. The Sherman was designed for mass production. It was also designed to be capable of being transported by road or rail to the ports of the USA, put in ships and carried all over the world, then landed if necessary over beaches into enemy territory. It then had to motor for miles without a breakdown while receiving the minimum of maintenance. All this it achieved with ease.

When the Sherman was first introduced in 1942 everyone sang its praises: 'We'll win the war with the M4' was the slogan heard everywhere. The British, who were the first to use the new tank in battle in North Africa, were positively euphoric about its performance:

Testimony by an Expert

'The M4 tank is a better tank than the best German tank,' is how British Generals described the Sherman to a party of senior American officers, led by General Devers, then Armored Force Commander, when they visited Montgomery's veteran Eighth Army. This was probably a perfectly true statement at the time, and indeed, later, when armoured units of the Eighth Army were withdrawn to the UK from Italy, prior to D-Day, and were re-equipped for the coming battle with the new British cruiser tank, the Cromwell, they were very unhappy. General Bobbie Erskine, GOC of the famous 7th Armoured Division (The Desert Rats) echoed these worries when he wrote later: '. . . It did not make matters easier when we found that the armoured brigade was to be equipped with Cromwells which was an entirely new tank for us. We all knew the Sherman inside out, but none of us knew the Cromwell. This had various repercussions. The armoured regiments had to learn the gunnery and maintenance of a new tank which many of them judged inferior to the Sherman.'[2]

One of the fairest assessments of the Sherman that I have read was written by the late General Mark Clark, commander of the US Fifth Army in Italy. To put his comments in

'The fustest with the mostest.' This cartoon appeared in the Washington DC Evening Star on 25 March 1945 and shows what cartoonist Berryman thought of the tank controversy (Tank Museum).

context, they were contained in a letter he wrote to Judge Jim Osborne of Vincennes, Indiana. Jim, as well as being a Judge in the Knox County Court, runs a fine military museum and amongst his vehicle collection is an immaculate M4A1E8(76)W, which you will see photographed from just about every angle later in this book. This is what General Clark had to say in answer to the question: 'How good was the Sherman?'

'All things considered, the M4 Sherman family of tanks were good tanks with your M4A3E8 being about the best of the breed. Perhaps the strongest point of the M4 was its manufacturing quality and quantity. Regardless of its design, the Sherman was a well finished and fitted tank. Further, over 40,000 were produced from 1943 to 1945. This was greater than the *total* of *all* German tracked vehicle production from 1934 to 1945. This quality and quantity were great advantages and helped outweigh some shortcomings.

'Unfortunately, the Sherman had more than its share of shortcomings. Its profile was far too high, its armor was woefully thin, and its gun was hopelessly underpowered. Interior stowage and access was poorly organized. The suspension gave a rough ride while the converted civilian engines were underpowered and tended to overheat. Both suspension and engine were difficult to maintain.

'On the strong side, the Sherman had excellent fire controls (sights and auxiliary systems) and superior gun controls (mechanisms for traversing and elevating). These items, coupled with the high finish quality of the weapons, allowed the American tanker to wring out the last ounce of potential firepower.

'Your M4A3E8 was an effort to improve upon the Sherman. Its thicker armor and bigger gun, while not enough (compared to German or Russian tanks) was a quantum leap over other models of the Sherman. Likewise, its new HVSS suspension and specially designed engine were vast improvements over earlier M4s. Since the M4A3E8 retained the other Sherman strong points, it was truly the best of the breed.

'Lastly, let me say a word about the American tanker. He was a highly trained and motivated individual. Gifted with innate American initiative and ingenuity, he took the organizational, technological and tactical expe-

dients necessary to capitalize on the Sherman's strong points and negate the effect of its weaknesses. It was this, coupled with the immense quantity of available replacement tanks, that made the Sherman an overwhelming force on the battlefield from 1943 to VE Day.'

No matter which way you look at it, a tank that can last for over 40 years and still be in service all over the world, has got to be counted as a success. Search now for the much vaunted Tigers and Panthers, and the only ones you will find are in museums, while the Sherman still soldiers on, getting the job done in an unspectacular yet businesslike way. As another of my correspondents, Les 'Spud' Taylor, who served with the Northamptonshire Yeomanry, put it when I asked him what he liked best about the Sherman: 'First, its utter mechanical reliability. Our one same vehicle carried us from the bocage through the chase to the River Seine, the battle for Le Havre, then by tank transporter through northern France and Belgium to the south of Holland. Defending the corridor Nijmegen-Eindhoven during Operation MARKET GARDEN, clearing the Noord Brabant, then the long cold winter journey to the Ardennes and the Battle of the Bulge. It says much for the expertise of our American friends that during the many battles and actions, plus the wear and tear of that long journey, I can only recall one breakdown, when the rubber stripped off a couple of bogie wheels. It never let us down during the fighting and apart from the laborious task of replenishing with ammunition and fuel, the usual checks were all that it required. The turret power traverse often gave us the edge over the hand-operated German types and, of course, being an American tank, it possessed an excellent toolkit.' Twenty-five years on, if you had asked an Israeli tanker on the Golan Heights for his comments, I have no doubt they would have been very similar.

This book is therefore a toast to a very fine piece of machinery, the M4 Sherman medium tank, and to all the tank crews of all the nations who have fought within its armoured frame over the past four decades.

George Forty,
Bryantspuddle,
Dorset,
December 1986.

ACKNOWLEDGEMENTS

As usual I have many people to thank for their invaluable help with the preparation of this book. First and foremost of course is John Batchelor, the well-known graphic artist, who has supplied most of the photographs I have used from his vast collection. All photographs not otherwise credited belong to him. Next, I must thank David Fletcher, Librarian at the Tank Museum, and Roland Groom, the Museum Photographer, for all their help. I am also indeed very fortunate to have such able and highly professional colleagues on my staff. I am of course very lucky to be sitting on top of one of the finest and most comprehensive libraries on armoured fighting vehicles in the world. We are also building up an unparalleled photographic collection at the Museum and vastly improving the cataloguing of photographs there so that they can be found quickly and easily. Finally, on the photographic side, I must thank my friend Judge Jim Osborne of the Indiana Military Museum, for allowing his immaculate Sherman to be used both on the cover and in the special Modeller's Annex; all the splendid photographs were taken by Bernie Schmitt. I am greatly indebted to them both.

I have many other individuals to thank on both sides of the Atlantic for their help with both stories and photographs; I will only attempt to name some of them and I hope anyone I have missed will not be offended. They are: General Bob Denig, USMC Ret, Colonels Owsley Costlow, Henry Gardiner and Dick Schmitt, Messrs Ed Bollard, Bill Haemmel, George Hofmann, Richard Hunnicutt, Paul Stevenson and Frank Woolner of the United States of America; Colonels Guy Daurel and Herve Doyen of France; Georges

Dummy Shermans came in all types of material – canvas and wood or even . . .

. a rubber dummy
herman!

Mazy of Belgium; Colonel David Eshel of Israel; General Pip Roberts, Group Captain Pat Hennessey, Colonel Tom Huggan, Messrs Bernard Cuttiford, Douglas Gardner, Christopher Foss, Albert Johnson, Bryan Perrett, George Stimpson and Spud Taylor of the UK.

Finally, I must thank my wife Anne, who once again, has nobly typed the manuscript. As she is now working full-time at the Tank Museum, and is largely responsible for all the marvellous new displays we are putting in there, she has to work on my books in her spare time and has devoted many hours to the unenviable task of reading my writing. Without her constant help and support this book would still be just another good idea.

TANK DESIGNATIONS

The system used to differentiate between newly designed prototypes, production models and later models of the same tank, was complicated and merits an early explanation. When a new tank was first designed, it was *designated* with a T (standing for Test) number, eg: the T6 was the designated test vehicle for the Sherman medium tank. After a wooden mockup had been made and approved, prototypes were built and tested – by the Ordnance for engineering purposes and by the users for tactical suitability (the Armored Board normally did this tactical testing). If the new tank proved satisfactory then it was *standardised,* which meant that the War Department approved its production and subsequent issue to units. Once standardised it was given an 'M' (standing for Model) number, eg: when it was standardised the T6 became the M4. As this example shows, new tanks did not necessarily keep the same number.

Major modifications/models of the same tank were indicated by the addition of the suffix 'A', plus a figure, eg: M4A2, M4A3, etc, for the various main production models of the Sherman. Minor modifications were indicated by the use of the suffix 'E', plus a figure, eg: M4A3E8 indicates that the tank is – M4, a Sherman; A3, it has had a major modification and E8, with HVSS (Horizontal Volute Spring Suspension) and wider tracks. Some types of weapons or special features were also shown, eg: '(76)' added to the Sherman model indicated that the main armament was a 76 mm gun instead of the original 75 mm, while the letter 'W' stood for wet stowage (a method of protecting ammunition in water jackets, to reduce fire risk). To add to the confusion, the British used their own system, which involved the use of the tank's nickname, such as Grant, Lee or Sherman, plus a figure, eg: a Sherman 2 was the British designation for the M4A1 medium tank. They also used a letter to describe the type of armament, eg: 'C' added to the Sherman model number denoted that it was armed with a 17-pdr gun.

EARLY INTEREST IN MEDIUMS

The aftermath of World War One left US Army tank units equipped with an odd assortment of obsolete tanks, such as the 6-ton light, based upon the French Renault FT 17 and the 38-ton Mark VIII, International, designed in cooperation with the British to fight the final battles of the war. The Tank Corps was officially disbanded in 1920, all existing tank units being assigned to the Infantry. Only very limited funds were made available for tank building, so that work had to be severely restricted even in the vital fields of research and development. This depressing situation was mirrored on the other side of the Atlantic, but at least in the British Army, the Tank Corps was able to retain its own individual identity. These retrograde and short-sighted decisions were to affect American tank development adversely for many years to come.

A year earlier, in 1919, while the Ordnance Department waited for the General Staff to announce its policy on postwar tank development, Major R. E. Carlson, an American member of the Anglo-American Tank Commission, made a complete survey of the situation and put forward recommendations on types of tanks for future development. His recommendations received the approval of both the Chief of the Tank Corps and the Chief of Infantry. As far as medium tanks were concerned, they called for a tank not more than 18 tons in weight, with a power-to-weight ratio of 10 hp/ton, a maximum cruising speed of 12 mph and a cruising range of 60 miles. Armament was to be a light cannon plus two machine-guns (MG), and it was to have sufficient armour to protect against close range .50-calibre armour piercing (AP) rounds. After approving these recommendations, the Ordnance Department was authorised to construct two pilot medium tanks, very similar in design to the Medium D, the last British tank to be designed before the end of the war.

The first pilot, the M1921, was completed at the Rock Island Arsenal in December 1921, and the second pilot, M1922, appeared the following year. M1921 weighed just over 18 tons (41,000 lb), was armed with a 16-pdr gun and had a four-man crew. M1922 was very similar, except that it had a flexible cable-type suspension. Testing soon revealed major engine problems and a new motor had to be developed by the Packard Motor Company. This work was successfully completed in 1925, when the new engine was installed into M1921. Other modifications were made at the same time and the tank redesignated as the Phase 1 Medium Tank, to be followed later by a Phase 2 model. The design features of the Phase 2 were incorporated into the Medium Tank T1, built in May 1927. Outwardly it still resembled the M1921, but it now weighed over 19 tons (43,900 lb), its 200 hp Packard engine giving it a power-to-weight ratio better than 10 hp/ton.

The medium tank T1 was also built at Rock Island. It incorporated improvements gleaned from trials of the M1921 and M1922. Outwardly it resembled the M1921 and was standardised as the Medium Tank M1 in February 1928, but it was withdrawn later that spring. It continued to be used for trials.

T2

In April 1922, the War Department at last published its policy on tank development for the next decade. Its relevance to the medium tank's development is such that it is worth repeating in full:

'1. The primary mission of the tank is to facilitate the uninterrupted advance of the riflemen in the attack. Its size, armament, speed and all accessories for making it an offensive force must be approached with above mission as the final objective to be obtained in development.

'2. As a matter of economy and simplicity in organisation, the number of types of tanks should be kept to a minimum. Reliance cannot be placed on a single type of tank, but two types, a light and a medium, should be capable of fulfilling all assigned missions.

'3. These types should be as follows:

(a) the light tank not exceeding 5 tons in weight and capable of being transported on heavy motor trucks.

(b) the medium tank not exceeding 15 tons in weight, thereby bringing it within the limits of average highway bridges, the capacity of railroads and the limit of 15 tons placed by the War Department on the medium pontoon bridge.

'4. Inasmuch as certain progress has already been made toward developing tanks of the medium type, first consideration should be given to that type, which is capable of doing all that is required of a light tank, except being transported in trucks. In the development of the medium tank, consideration should be given to the essentials necessary to make it a fighting machine. Its speed should be the greatest possible consistent with the limitation in weight, economy in fuel and radius of action. The control of speed should permit reduction to that of the advancing rifleman.

'5. The armament of medium tanks should consist of machine-guns and guns of heavier calibre. The guns should be capable of firing upon enemy troops in trenches, and engage enemy tanks on a basis of equality; they should therefore be of as large calibre as is consistent with prescribed weight limits and ammunition supply, but no necessity is seen for high angle fire. The radius of action, vision and manoeuverabilities of tanks should permit complete fulfillment of the assigned mission. These essentials should be determined after a thorough study and experiment and concur-rent with the development of pilot tanks. Auxiliary vehicles, except signal tanks, should not be of a type special to the tank service alone.

'6. The tank is not likely to decrease in importance as a war weapon, but tank construction is expensive and it must be expected that funds will be limited. It is, therefore, directed that developments be conducted along the following lines:

a. The Chief of Ordnance will be allowed great latitude in the development of pilot tanks for test purposes, in close cooperation with the Chief of Infantry.

b. The first program will be the development of suitable medium pilot tanks with their equipment, of a weight not exceeding 15 tons, and of a maximum speed of not less than twelve miles per hour.

c. That for the present funds and effort will be applied principally to development purposes rather than to the construction of complete tank units.

d. The manufacture of complete tank units will not be undertaken until suitable medium pilot tanks have been developed and have been approved by the War Department as the best type available.

e. Tanks will not be designed with special adaptation to chemical warfare, except that if it be found practible to do so the tanks should be made gas-proof and supplied with a means of producing non-toxic smoke clouds. In this development, the Chief Chemical Warfare Service, will be consulted.

f. The development of special auxiliary vehicles for tank service alone will not be undertaken; but there is no objection to the consideration of general special purpose vehicles capable of meeting the general needs of the Army, as well as the special requirements for tanks.

g. Expenditure of funds on existing tanks will be limited to the amount necessary to keep those in actual service in repair and those in storage from deterioration.'[3]

The imposition of the 15-ton weight limit made a radical change to the policy agreed already between the Ordnance and Infantry, virtually scrapping all the work which had been done so far on the Medium tank T1. It also gave fresh impetus to a new design study known as the Model 1924 which was to weigh under 15 tons. Limited funds held up its construction until 1929, by which time its

outward appearance had changed so radically that it now resembled the contemporary British Vickers Medium Mark II, with a front-mounted engine. It was designated the T2, had a laden weight of just under 14 tons (31,200 lb), was powered by a 338 hp Liberty engine, giving it a power-to-weight ratio of some 24 hp/ton and a top speed of 20-25 mph. Completed in 1930, T2 was armed with a 47 mm gun and a coaxially mounted .50 Browning Heavy MG in the turret, plus a 37 mm gun and coax .30 BMG in the right bow. This latter mount soon proved troublesome and was replaced by a single .30 MG, a further .30 MG being added on an AA mount on top of the turret. Although it did not meet Carlson's original requirements as far as assured protection was concerned, T2 was still the best of the mediums so far designed, with a good cross-country performance, a fair turn of speed and excellent firepower. However, limited funds were to prevent its production.

CHRISTIE CONVERTIBLES

In parallel with the development of T1 and T2 was the work done by the brilliant, but unpredictable, J. Walter Christie, using his unique suspension, with its large wheels and removable steel tracks. The reasoning behind wanting to be able to remove the tracks and run on the suspension wheels alone was based on World War One experience. It had been found that many tanks were likely to break down with track faults well before they went into action and, while tank transporters could be provided, they were expensive and increased bridging and other movement problems. If, however, the tracks could be removed easily and the armoured fighting vehicle (AFV) run on its wheels up to the Start Line where its tracks could be quickly replaced, then these problems would be overcome. The Christie Medium M1919 was armed with a 6-pdr gun and a coaxially-mounted .30 MG in a round turret. It weighed about 12 tons, was powered by a 120 hp engine and its suspension consisted of four large unsprung roadwheels, fitted with rubber tyres. In between the roadwheels was a two wheel bogie with large coil springs. These bogies were raised when running without tracks.

M1919 was tested at Aberdeen Proving Ground (APG) between 1919 and 1921, when the programme was suspended so that various modifications could be made. The tank returned to APG in March 1922, now redesignated as the M1921 and looking very different. The turret had been removed, the crew enlarged to four and the suspension altered significantly, with two large roadwheels on a pivoting bogie replacing the two-wheel bogie. The two front roadwheels were sprung with large coil springs but the rear wheels remained unsprung, drive being to these two wheels only. Manoeuvrability proved to be poor and the tank was also mechanically unreliable, so it was rejected after trials.

Christie now turned to the development of a new, lightweight, high-speed chassis, designated as the M1928, although it was also called the M1940 as Christie reckoned it was so far ahead of its time! It weighed only 8.6 tons, yet was powered by a 338 hp engine, giving it a top speed on roads, on its wheels, of 70 mph and over 42 mph on its tracks. Its suspension consisted of four independently-sprung road wheels on either side of the chassis. After prolonged testing Christie was given a contract to build first one, then a further six of these high speed tanks, now called the M1931. The first was delivered to APG in October 1931 and

Convertible medium tank T3, seen here on its wheels, about to run on to its tracks. Produced in 1931, it typifies Christie's high speed AFVs, with four large wheels on either side, mounted on arms connected to large vertical, hull-mounted adjustable springs. Note the shelf above the wheels on which to stow the tracks.

officially designated as the Convertible Medium Tank T3. It had a laden weight of 9.8 tons, a top speed on its wheels of over 46 mph and on its tracks of 27 mph; however, it was governed down to 40 mph and 25 mph respectively. Three of the new tanks, armed with a 37 mm gun and a .30 coaxial MG, were sent to serve with the 67th Infantry (Medium Tanks) at Fort Benning, Georgia, while the other four were assigned to the Cavalry at Fort Knox, Kentucky, and armed with a heavy .50 MG in place of the 37 mm cannon. These four had to be designated as 'Combat Cars', in view of the crazy regulations then in force, that only the Infantry were able to have tanks. The most recognisable feature of the convertible T3 was its sloping, pointed frontal armour which was between $\frac{3}{8}$ and $\frac{1}{2}$ inch thick.

Further testing and modification of the convertible T3 led to production of the T3E2 and the T3E3, then finally to the T4, the last medium to be built based upon Christie's convertible design. Sixteen T4s were produced between 1935 and 1936, the largest quantity tank production in the USA since the end of World War One. T4 had a four-man crew, weighed $13\frac{1}{2}$ tons and had a power-to-weight ratio of 19.8 hp/ton from its 268 hp Continental engine. It had a two-man turret with a .50 HMG and coaxial .30 MG, the other two crew being in the hull, the bow gunner operating a .30 MG. Top speed was 37.8 mph on wheels and 23.9 mph on tracks.

The T4 and T4E1 were both designated as the Convertible Medium Tank M1 on standardisation in 1939, some 18 being in service when they were declared obsolete in 1940. The basic problem with the convertibles was the fact that their firepower was only on a par with the M2 light tank, yet they cost twice as much to build. As firepower is the most important characteristic of a tank's main attributes – the other two being protection and mobility – then clearly this was unacceptable.

The Ordnance history sums up the feelings about the Christie tanks as follows: '... most Ordnance officers remained skeptical, believing that the speed of the Christie failed to compensate for its light armor, light firepower, inability to make long runs without overhaul, and lack of room inside for guns, radio and ammunition'.

T5 AND M2

Neither Christie nor his revolutionary designs had found much favour in the USA and it was left to Britain with its cruiser range, and Russia with its BT1 series, to make the most of his suspension system. In America it was decided to revert to more conventional lines with the design of the next medium, the T5. Essentially, the new tank was an enlarged version of the M2 light tank and shared many of its features and components, being powered, for example, by the same 250 hp Continental radial engine. It also had similar vertical volute suspension, sprockets, tracks and transmission. T5 was completed in early 1938 and brought to APG for testing in mid-February. The tank had a five-man crew, weighed just over 15 tons, had a top speed of 31 mph and a radius of action of 125 miles. It was armed with a 37 mm gun in the turret, four flexibly-mounted .30 MG in small sponsons on each corner of the barbette around the turret, plus two fixed .30 MG in the front of the hull. Trials soon proved that the T5 was underpowered, so it was re-engined with a 350 hp Wright nine-cylinder air-cooled radial engine and redesignated as the T5 Phase III. Further trials proved successful and the tank was standardised as the Medium Tank M2, in June 1939, the first tank to be standardised since 1919. Production of 15 M2s began in August 1939, a further two .30 MG being added to the sides of the turret in the production model.

The medium tank T5E2 was the Phase 3 model into which had been installed a 75 mm pack howitzer. Note the rangefinder in the small six-sided cupola (plus MG) replacing the turret. This was the test vehicle for the medium tank M3 Lee/Grant.

The medium tank M2 was standardised in June 1939. Fifteen were built at Rock Island in 1939, with a further 54 authorised for 1940; however, these were cancelled.

The medium tank T5 (Phase 3) was the pilot tank for the M2 medium tank. It was similar to the Phase 1 model but had a larger 350 hp Wright radial air-cooled engine and wider tracks. It was the basis of this design that would be developed and refined to produce the M2, M3 and finally the M4 Sherman.

Internal views of the driving and fighting compartments of the M2 medium tank.

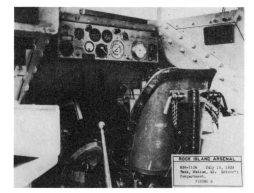

Views through the open rear doors of the 350 hp Wright nine-cylinder, air-cooled radial engine as fitted to the M2. It was later uprated for the M2A1.

The 37 mm gun mount M19, complete with telescope, as fitted in both the M2 and M2A1.

The medium tank M2A1 was almost identical to the M2 except it had thicker armour (1¼ inches) and a larger turret. Engine was the uprated 400 hp model. Altogether 1,000 were ordered but under 100 were actually built, as the order was cancelled in favour of the M3.

M2A1

The following year an improved version, the M2A1, was developed, with a wider turret, thicker armour, wider tracks and better sighting gear. The engine had a supercharger fitted to uprate it to 400 hp. The M2A1 was scheduled to go into quantity production at the still to be completed new Detroit Tank Arsenal, an order for some 1,000 having been placed in early August 1940. However, study of the first tank battles of the war in Poland and France had quickly convinced everyone that they must be aiming for a tank that could match the highly successful German PzKpfw IIIs and IVs, beside which the M2A1 was both under-gunned and underarmoured. To survive on the modern battlefield a tank clearly needed a powerful gun with dual capability, that is to say, the ability to fire both armour-piercing (AP) and high explosive (HE) ammunition. The AP had to be large enough in calibre to penetrate the armour of all potential enemy tanks, while the HE was necessary to deal quickly with anti-tank gun crews. At meetings held that August between the Chief of the newly-formed Armored Force and the Ordnance Department, it was decided that 75 mm was the right calibre of tank gun to go for, although there was only limited experience of mounting such a large gun in a tank turret.

However, in 1938 trials had taken place with a 75 mm howitzer being mounted in the right front of the hull of the Medium T5 Phase III model. Based upon the success of that trial it was decided to opt for mounting the new gun in a sponson on the right-hand side of the tank, reminiscent of the way in which such guns had been mounted in the heavy tanks of World War One. The now familiar silhouette of the M3 was thus poised to go on to the drawing board for the very first time. The acceptance of the yet-undesigned M3 medium tank signalled the end of the M2A1 and the planned contract for 1,000 M2A1s was cancelled on 28 August 1940, the new medium being substituted. As Wesley W. Stout explained in his book about the achievements of the Chrysler Corporation in World War Two, entitled *Tanks are Mighty Fine Things*: '... The Chrysler tank contract began with an order dated August 15 1940, for

Internal view of the fighting compartment of the M2A1, showing the radio installation on the rear turret wall.

Sponson mount for the .30-calibre Browning machine-gun on M2A1. Note that each sponson has its own telescope.

1,000 M2A1 23 ton tanks to be delivered by August 1942, at the rate of 100 per month. It specified that the arsenal was to be completed by September 1941. Thirteen days after the contract was placed, Ordnance scrapped the M2A1 design and substituted the 28 ton M3, as yet undesigned. Yet Chrysler made the first two M3 pilot tanks in April 1941, and made its first production tank in July, had delivered more than 500 before Pearl Harbor and all of the first 1,000 by January 26 1942, eight months ahead of schedule.'

Despite this major change of heart a few M2A1s were ordered to be built by the Rock Island Arsenal, which completed 94 up to August 1941. These tanks, and the M2s left in service, were used only for training and trials, which included tests with the E2 Flame Gun and M3 turret installation. The M2A1 thus did useful service despite its obsolesence and assisted in training the new Armored Force. Both the M2 and M2A1 were finally declared obsolete in late 1942.

BUYERS FROM BRITAIN

The success of the German Panzer divisions in France in the spring of 1940 had brought the tank into prominence as the most important weapon of ground warfare and had emphasised the need for Britain to equip more armoured divisions. However, there was a desperate shortage of tanks, due to the losses in France, and it was clear that the AFVs needed to make up for these losses and to equip the additional armoured divisions, just could not be produced fast enough in Great Britain. Accordingly, the British Government turned to the United States and Canada for assistance. At first the British Purchasing Commission in America was merely seeking firms to build British-designed tanks or to supply components for tanks under construction in the UK. At the time of the defeat of France in June 1940, the Commission had hardly scratched the surface, having placed only a handful of orders with individual companies. The vast American automotive and railway industries were still making peacetime products and had not yet been turned over to the production of armoured vehicles. The Commission, in June 1940, put forward the suggestion that tank deliveries would be much faster if the British adopted American designs, or encouraged the Americans to accept British or French designs. Clearly, with the huge expansion which full-time tank production would bring in its wake, the former solution was the more sensible, but the matter was a very complex one. It was therefore decided to send out a special mission to the United States, under a man of wide engineering business and administrative experience, who also had American business connections. This man was Mr Michael Dewar, and he and his team arrived in New York on 29 July 1940.[4] He had long been an advocate of building large numbers of tanks and had expressed his views to the Prime Minister on more than one occasion, so he was the ideal choice to lead the team.

STARTING FROM SCRATCH

In July 1940, the US defence programme was just beginning to take shape and it is relevant here to look briefly at the way in which, after years of vacillation and inactivity, America was able so quickly to grasp the urgency of the situation and to bring its massive resources of men and material into action, to design, build and equip the new industry that would be needed to produce the tanks, guns, ships, aircraft and all the rest of the complex hardware that modern warfare demands. Taking Chrysler as an example – most appropriate as they were destined to build the M3 and its successors – the situation in 1940 was that most of their workforce had never even seen a tank at close quarters, let alone knew how to build one. It was necessary to send their engineers to the Rock Island Arsenal, to look at tanks and tank models, and to obtain the large quantities of blueprints from which they would have to work. As the Ordnance history explains, once the preliminary visits had been made, '... Back in Detroit on 17 June, they began intensive work, behind closed doors, estimating the costs of buildings, machines and materials. They worked from early morning until late at night, seven days a week. Finally on 17 July, Keller delivered his completed estimate to Knudsen in Washington. A tank arsenal to produce ten medium tanks a day would cost $21 million and each tank (complete except for guns) would cost about $30,000.' These figures were based upon the original M2A1 and more frantic work had to take place in order to modify and modernise the design. However, while this was going on the new tank arsenal, where the first 1,000 medium tanks of the new M3 design would be produced, had to be built, so they were, in effect, attempting to do the development work, build the new facilities and go into production all at the same time!

'The contract signed, and a 100 acre tract of farmland on the outskirts of Detroit selected as the site, ground for the new tank arsenal was broken early in September 1940. A Chrysler engineer was meanwhile sent to Aberdeen where designs of the new M3 were coming off the drawing boards. He mailed copies of blueprints to Detroit, relayed other information by telephone, and along with representatives of the railway equipment companies offered Ordnance designers valuable suggestions on engineering changes that would mean cheaper and faster production. Late in January the steel of the main arsenal building was up, and in mid-April 1941, the first tank was presented to Ordnance as the gift of Chrysler dealers throughout the country. By July, Keller wrote to Under Secretary Patterson that the tank arsenal was "beginning to look like a producing department" and would turn out 507 tanks during the next five months.'[5]

Of course Detroit could not handle all the demands for new tanks, even for mediums, so Ordnance placed additional orders for M3 medium tanks with the American Locomotive Company (for 685) and with the Baldwin Locomotive Works (for 535) bringing the total orders up to 2,220. In addition, the British contracted directly with Baldwin, Lima Locomotive Works and the Pullman Standard Car Company for more mediums, while the Canadian government did likewise with the Montreal division of the American Locomotive Company, for 1,157 tanks of the M3 design. The United States, not unnaturally, refused to allow the British to place contracts with American firms to build British-designed tanks, making them accept the M3 for both British and Canadian forces, albeit, as we shall see, with certain modifications, and this greatly simplified both production and maintenance.

ONLY AN INTERIM MODEL

From the outset, the M3 medium was never thought of as being anything other than a stopgap, as one American officer put it: '... As far as it is humanly possible to say, the design is right and settled. This design is based on our best engineering knowledge, but I do not believe we have ever built a tank or anything else that did not have to be altered at first.'[6] The M3 medium tank was standardised on 11 July 1940 and production ordered long before the design was actually finalised, so the summer months of 1940 saw considerable changes taking place to the original concept which had been merely to up-armour the M2A1 and put a

75 mm gun into the front right side of the hull. When the wooden mockup of the new tank was unveiled, the main gun had been installed in a sponson turret with limited traverse, the gun being a short-barrelled version of the T6 low-velocity anti-aircraft gun, which had been redesignated as the 75 mm gun T7. To make up for the loss of the right front sponson machine-gun, there was a small auxiliary turret on the left front of the hull with two .30 MG. The 37 mm gun of the M2A1 had been retained and mounted in a turret on top of the hull, together with a coaxially-mounted .30 MG. Finally, on top of this turret there was a large cupola containing yet another .30 MG, designed for AA use by the commander.

Any tankman looking at the new design could immediately see its major weaknesses – the limited traverse and low positioning of the 75 mm main gun, which meant that a very large proportion of the tank had to be exposed when bringing the gun into action. In a hull-down fire position one tries to keep as much of the tank as possible behind the slope, to lessen the silhouette and gain as much protection as one can from the ground. In addition, all-round traverse is vital. However, Ordnance had no experience of mounting such a large gun in a

Front view of the wooden mockup of the final design for the M3 medium tank.

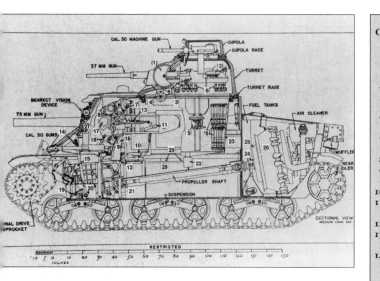

Cutaway drawing of the Lee, taken from the Technical Manual (Tank Museum).

Ammunition stowage and weapons of the M3 Lee (Tank Museum).

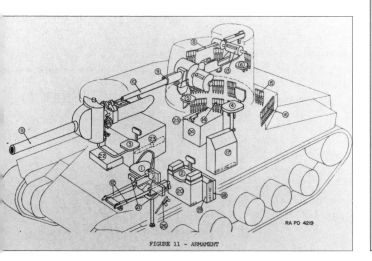

FIGURE 11 - ARMAMENT

fully rotating turret. The Armored Force felt so strongly about these drawbacks as to suggest that the production of the M3 be limited drastically until a proper turret could be designed for the 75 mm gun, but the demand was so urgent, especially among the British, that this delay was obviously unacceptable and full production had to begin as soon as possible. Ordnance did, however, promise to start work immediately on the design of a new tank which would carry a 75 mm gun in a fully rotating turret.

One of the major modifications made to the original mockup was the removal of all the sponson-mounted machine-guns and their sponsons, still leaving the tank with the not inconsiderable armament of one 75 mm gun, one 37 mm gun and four .30 MG. Other modifications agreed at this time (August 1940) were: moving the radio set to the left front sponson, where the auxiliary turret had been located; increasing the size of the fuel tanks; lowering the floor of the turret to give more room; installing pistol ports strategically around the tank; and providing better vision devices, seats, etc, for the crew. The wooden mockup was rebuilt to incorporate these changes and accepted.

THE BRITISH VERSION

As has been explained, the British Tank Mission headed by Michael Dewar was looking for suitable tanks to purchase. They were interested in the new medium, but did not like the turret arrangement, or the fact that the radio was in the hull. They preferred to have the radio in the turret, so that the 37 mm loader could double up as radio operator and they would thus be able to manage with one less crew member, an important factor in a country where manpower was limited.[7] It was therefore agreed to design a special turret for the British, which was slightly lower but larger in diameter than the US one, with a rear bustle for the radio and no cupola, thus reducing the height of the tank. The design was undertaken by Mr L. E. Carr, the design expert of the Tank Mission, with the assistance of the General Steel Castings Corporation, who produced the turrets. The British version of the M3, incorporating these modifications, was known as the General Grant, after the famous Union leader of the American Civil War, General Ulysses S. Grant, whilst the original version, with its machine-gun cupola, became known as the General Lee, after Grant's Confederate opponent, General Robert E. Lee. As Richard P. Hunnicutt comments in his book *Sherman* (undoubtedly the finest and most comprehensive work of reference on the American medium tank ever written): '... The British designation for their version of the M3 was the General Grant 1. The standard US model was referred to as the General Lee. It was obvious which one they considered the winner.'

Rear of Grant, showing bustle on rear of British turret (where the wireless set was located) and rear engine doors open, giving access to the engine for maintenance (Tank Museum).

Other modifications included:

a. Installing a transmission oil cooler (situated on the engine compartment bulkhead) to prevent the driver getting severe burns off the hot casing. The Americans later adopted the same scheme for their tanks.

b. Internal fittings for proper combat stowage, such as ammo boxes, water containers, map cases, oil cans, boxes for spares for the periscopes and guns, boxes for greatcoats and tin hats, fire extinguishers, first aid kits, etc (also eventually adopted by the Americans once they appreciated the need for these fittings to make a tank ready for battle).

c. Splash proofing, namely the protection of the ports to prevent splash from the impact of bullets entering and injuring the crew.

London gave its blessing to the procurement of the modified M3 tanks but the quantity to be ordered gave some problems. Initially the authority was for only 1,000 of the modified M3, which after further consideration, Dewar requested increasing to 1,250. However, in subsequent discussions with the Americans, it became clear that unless a firm British order for at least 3,000 tanks was placed, it would be impossible to build up the desired production capacity of 20 tanks a day, or even to find capacity that was not already occupied to the limit by the United States' own requirements. Either the British had to order 3,000 tanks at once or run the risk of slow deliveries which would cease entirely after the manufacture of

1,500. This put the Ministry of Supply and the War Office in a difficult situation, having to accept a double order of a design with which they already had misgivings. They stipulated, therefore, that while they agreed that the requirement to order 3,000 tanks should be met solely with American type tanks, they would not be committed to taking more than 1,500 M3s. They believed, and of course events proved them correct, that long before all the M3s had been delivered, the urgent need for an improved tank would be clear to everyone and that production would change over to the new model.

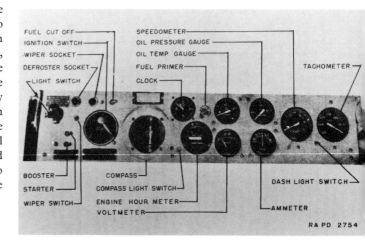

GENERAL DESCRIPTION

The Technical Manual for the Medium Tank M3, described it as being: '. . . an armored, full track-laying vehicle, powered by a nine-cylinder, air-cooled radial aircraft type engine located in the rear of the hull. The operator steers the vehicle by means of two levers located in the front of the hull. The vehicle has five forward speeds and one reverse. The tank is wired for radio installation and for an interphone system within the tank. The armor plate is considerably thicker than on previous medium tanks. The armor on the front upper section, cupola and turret sides is 2 inches thick; the armor on the sides of the hull and the front section is $1\frac{1}{2}$ inches thick. The turret is 60 inches in diameter and can be rotated by means of a hydraulic system, or by hand. The cupola normally rotates with the turret but can be rotated independently by hand. There is an auxiliary electrical generating system in the tank, consisting of a generating set powered by a single cylinder gasoline engine. This unit heats the engine in cold weather and also charges the batteries.'[8]

In general terms, the M3 was very simple in design, with a large, roomy crew/fighting compartment which housed the driver's position, the 75 mm gun sponson and crew, the turret basket and the transmission housing. The last of these was to the right of the driver's position and took up a fair amount of room. It was needed to house the transmission which ran under the floor from the centre of the rear-mounted radial engine, to the gearbox at the front of the tank beside the driver. It was the need to run this transmission through the tank which really dictated the height of the M3.

DRIVING POSITION AND CONTROLS

The driver sat in the left front of the crew compartment with his instrument panel located directly below his vision port. Panel instruments included: speedometer (with integral mileage counter), rev counter, ammeter, voltmeter, oil pressure gauge, temperature gauge and clock. His main controls were: a foot accelerator pedal (located to the right of the transmission housing, convenient to the driver's right foot); a hand-operated throttle (mounted on the floor to the driver's right and to the right of the gear shift lever); two steering levers (mounted on the floor one each side of the driver's seat. Pulling back on either one slowed down the track on that side, while the speed of the other track increased, thus the tank turned with power on both tracks at all times. The levers had rubber grips, also switches to fire the two fixed machine guns in the front plate of the tank. Pulling back simultaneously on both steering levers slowed down and stopped the tank, depending upon the effort applied); parking brake lever (located on the left, behind the steering lever. It was a transmission type brake and only for use when parking); a clutch pedal (located to the left of the transmission housing, convenient to the driver's left foot); gearshift lever (to the driver's right, with five forward, neutral and reverse positions, with a latch to prevent accidental shifting from first into reverse and vice versa).

MAIN ARMAMENT

The tank's main gun, the 75 mm M2 or M3 in the mount M1, was mounted in its side sponson which had some 30° of traverse (15° left

Driver's instrument panel on the M3 (Tank Museum).

and right) and 29° of elevation (from −9° to +20°). The 75 mm gunner sat to the right rear of the driver and his loader stood to the left rear of the breech of the gun. The 75 mm gun was originally the T7, which could claim to be descended from the famous French 75 mm gun which had been adopted by the US Army in 1918. The T7 was standardised as the 75 mm gun M2 and the hull mounting designated as the 75 mm gun mount M1. This first version had a barrel 84 inches long, a muzzle velocity of 1,860 fps, and was equipped with a semi-automatic vertical sliding breechblock. A later improved model of the gun, the M3, had a 110 inch-long barrel and an increased muzzle velocity of 2,300 fps.

The tank was fitted with gyrostabilisation for both the 75 mm and 37 mm guns, in elevation only. It was the first tank ever to be fitted with a mass-produced stabiliser (from July 1941) made by the Westinghouse Company. These were early days for stabilisation and the 'state of the art' had not reached anything like that on modern tank gunnery systems. However, the principle was exactly the same, namely, to maintain the bore of the gun at a given elevation, no matter what the gyrations of the tank were as it moved across rough country. In theory this enabled accurate shooting on the move, in practice at least it allowed the gunner to keep roughly aligned on his target whilst on the move, so as to speed up any resulting engagement when the tank halted. The fitting of the stabiliser for use with both types of 75 mm gun meant that their difference in barrel length/weight had to be compensated. Thus, in order to make up for the lower barrel weight when the M2 gun was fitted into a tank set up for an M3 gun, a large counterweight had to be added to the end of the barrel.

The gun was layed on to a target by means of an M1 periscope which incorporated a telescopic sight and was mounted in the roof of the sponson. The sight had an adjustable vertical graticule and fixed horizontal graticule pattern representing ranges from 0 to 3,000 yards (3,500 yards on later sights with the M3 gun). Gun controls comprised: a geared elevation handwheel (one complete revolution = 1° 18′), a traverse handwheel, with a firing button in the centre of the wheel. The gun was normally fired electrically with a solenoid switch operating the firing trigger, but there was also a manual (mechanical) firing device which was operated by a button directly in front of the gunner, located above the traversing hand-wheel. Later, a foot switch was fitted to fire the solenoid. A total of 50 rounds of 75 mm ammunition was carried, 41 in boxes on the floor of the crew compartment, right side, directly behind the 75 mm gun. The remaining nine were in portable cartons as ready rounds. Ammunition was either AP M61, AP Mark IT, SAP M72, HE Mark 1 normal, HE M48 Supercharge, or Smoke. Maximum firing rate for the 75 mm was 20 rounds per minute.

TURRET ARMAMENT

The fully traversing turret with 37 mm M5 or M6 gun and coaxial .30 MG in a M24 Mount was offset to the left-hand side of the tank and its turret basket took up a large amount of the space inside the crew compartment. Three members of the crew were inside this basket, with their seats fixed to the sides of the turret cage. These were the commander, 37 mm gunner and loader. The gunner sat on the left with the loader beside him on the right (in the Grant the loader doubled as radio operator), and the tank commander sat behind them and to the left. In the Lee, the commander had a separate rotating cupola, which incorporated a .30 Browning MG and three protectorscopes and added about four inches to the height of the tank. In the Grant he merely had a circular hatch, with a split hinged lid with a single periscope incorporated into it, so that he could see when the hatch was closed down. Also in the Grant the radio was set in the turret bustle, behind the commander, while outside was a two-inch bomb thrower (as found on most British tanks), plus a pintle mounting on the ring of the commander's hatchway so that a Browning MG could be fitted.

The gunner's controls comprised: manual and powered traverse controllers, the former being worked with his left hand, while he operated the spade grip for the latter with his right. Close to his left hand was the system selector lever. It was possible to traverse through 360° in 20 seconds using power and the firing switches for both the 37 mm gun and .30 MG were mounted on the powered traverse controller; an elevating handwheel was located on the left side of the 37 mm gun directly in front of the gunner. Turning the handwheel counterclockwise depressed the guns to a maximum of −7° while turning clockwise elevated them up to a maximum of

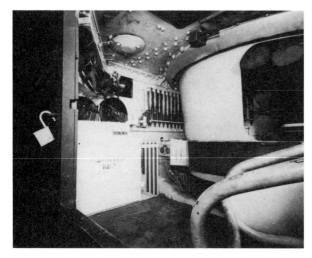
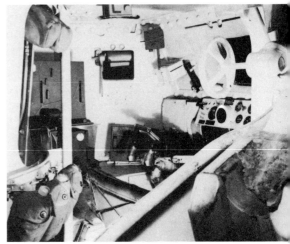

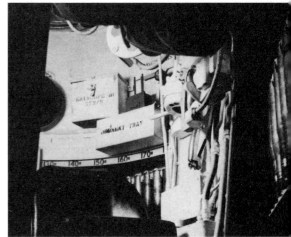

Six good internal shots
of the M3 medium tank
showing stowage in hull
and turret.

28

+60°. The guns were fired electrically by squeezing the safety grip and depressing the switches on the powered traverse controller. Care had to be exercised to ensure that the loader's hand was not caught in the gun's automatic breechblock. The sighting equipment on the 37 mm gun combination mount was of the periscopic type similar to that used with the 75 mm gun, but with a different graticule pattern which incorporated ranges from 0 to 1,500 yards for the 37 mm gun and 0 to 1,000 yards for the MG. The sight display was a circle with a dot in the middle, which also acted as a battle sight for both guns. The maximum rate of fire for the 37 mm gun was 30 rounds per minute, 178 rounds being carried, some inside the turret walls in racks as ready rounds, and others in boxes in the turret and elsewhere.

OTHER ARMAMENT

The additional machine-guns have all been mentioned; all were .30-calibre Browning M1919A4 MGs. The cupola-mounted MG in the Lee was traversed by rotating the cupola and could be elevated between $-8\frac{1}{2}°$ and +60°; the bow guns were located in the left side of the driver's compartment, projecting through the front plate, and fired by the driver. In later models only one was fitted. Tripods were carried for external use of the bow MGs, while a total of 9,200 rounds of .30-calibre ammunition was carried for use by all MGs. One or two Thompson .45-calibre sub-machine-guns were normally carried in the fighting compartment to be used through the pistol ports and 1,200 rounds of .45 calibre were carried, plus 12 hand grenades.

RADIO INSTALLATIONS

In the Lee the normal radio (located in the front left sponson) was the SCR 508 transceiver (early models had the SCR 245); in command tanks an SCR 506 was located in the right rear sponson; Interphone (part of the radio) comprised five stations in various parts of the tank and all crew members had earphones. In the Grant, the British Wireless Set No 19 was fitted (in the turret bustle). It comprised an A set for long range work, a B set for troop communications and IC to operate as for the Interphone.

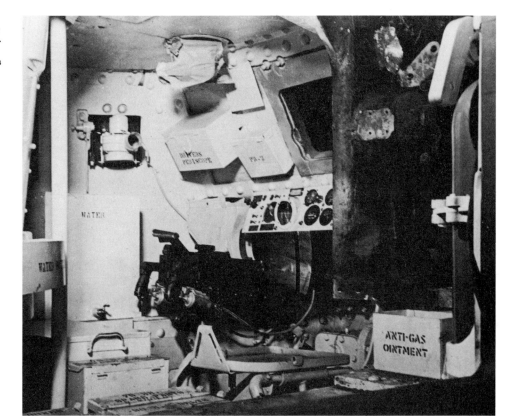

ft side of the driving
npartment, showing
e twin fixed machine-
ns, which fired
rough the front glacis
te (Tank Museum).

AUXILIARY GENERATING UNIT

Located in the left rear corner of the fighting compartment, on a level with the turret deck, was the auxiliary generator, a self-contained generating unit for charging the tank batteries (and thus running all the electrical components on the tank such as the power traverse, stabiliser, etc), and for preheating the tank engine compartment in cold weather. It could also be used for heating the crew compartment. It consisted of a single-cylinder air-cooled petrol engine, a 30 V 1,500 W generator, a blower and a heater duct running to the engine compartment. It had its own fuel tank in the left sponson, which held $2\frac{1}{2}$ gallons of a mixture of petrol and oil.

ENGINE COMPARTMENT

The layout of the engine compartment differed with the type of engine fitted – initially the engine fitted in all models was the nine-cylinder Wright (Continental) R975 EC2 petrol engine, but the M3A3 model had the 12-cylinder General Motors 6046 diesel water-cooled engine, while the M3A4 and M3A5 were fitted with the 30-cylinder Chrysler A37 Multibank petrol engine. Four fuel tanks (two vertical in the front corners of the engine compartment and two larger horizontal tanks on either side) gave a total capacity of 175 gallons (slightly less on later models). Access to the engine for daily maintenance was via the rear hull doors and it was possible to do most things through this opening. A major repair, however, or an engine change, required the removal of the rear armoured decking. Cooling for the Continental EC2 radial was by air, so the engine compartment had to be large enough to allow air to circulate properly. The air blast was produced by a fan mounted on the flywheel, which drew air through a grille in the top of the hull and forced it down and around the finned cylinders of the engine. The warm air passed out through a screen above the engine doors on the rear of the tank. The GM 6046 and Chrysler Multibank were both liquid-cooled engines. Power from the engine was transmitted via the clutch, which was built into the engine flywheel and located on the front of the engine, to the gearbox at the front of the tank via the propeller shaft, and thence to the differential, final drives and sprockets.

TRACKS AND SUSPENSION

Six two-wheeled rubber-tyred bogies (three

Fitters at work on the radial engine of an M3 Grant. The engine weighed 1,137 lb, so lifting gear was essential.

New tracks being fitted to a Lee belonging to the 8th Princess Louise (New Brunswick) Hussars of Canada, while on training in UK June 1942.

each side), bolted to the hull, supported the tank on springs. This was the similar vertical volute suspension as found on the light tank series and on the M2 and M2A1 medium tanks. The tracks were driven by front-mounted sprockets, while two adjustable idlers at the rear end of the hull provided a means of ensuring constant tension on the tracks. The weight of the upper portion of track was carried by six single steel track supporting rollers, one on top of each of the suspension brackets. There were 158 track links (79 in each track) giving a ground contact length of 147 inches (166 links and 160 inches for the M3A4). Track width was 16 inches.

MODELS AND SPECIFICATIONS

There were basically six different models of the M3, details of which are shown in the table on this page. It is also necessary to differentiate

MODELS OF THE M3 MEDIUM TANK		
Model	**Remarks**	**Numbers built**
M3	The initial production model, with riveted hull, side doors and Wright radial engine.	4,924 – Apr 1941 to Aug 1942
M3A1	Cast instead of riveted hull, otherwise identical to M3 but later production models had no side doors or hull floor escape hatch.	300 – Feb to Aug 1942
M3A2	All welded hull and cast turret.	12 only – Jan to Mar 1942
M3A3	Fitted with twin GM diesel engines which increased performance, but put up weight to 63,000 lb. Designation later restricted to vehicles with welded hulls.	322 – Mar to Dec 1942
M3A4	Identical to M3, but with Chrysler 370 hp A 57 Multibank engine, which comprised five commercial truck engines coupled together on a common drive shaft. Weight increased to 64,000 lb; hull just over one foot longer, as were chassis and tracks. It had no side doors.	109 – Jun to Aug 1942
M3A5	As for M3A3 but with riveted hull. No side doors on late production models.	591 – Jan to Nov 1942

initial production
del of the M3, with
ted hull and side
nson doors. It was
ered by the Wright
e-cylinder
tinental R975 EC2
cooled radial engine.

between the nicknames Lee and Grant, detailed in the next table, below.

Specifications did, of course, vary with the model and unfortunately space does not allow me to cover all models so I have chosen three examples, the original Lee and Grant, plus the M3A5.

NICKNAMES

Grant I	The M3 with turret designed to British requirements.
Grant II	British designation for M3A5 with original American turret.
Lee I	British designation for M3.
Lee II	Designation for M3A1.
Lee III	Designation for M3A2 (none delivered to the British).
Lee IV	Designation for M3A3 with Continental engine.
Lee V	Designation for diesel-engined M3A3.
Lee VI	Designation for M3A4.

The M3A1 model had a cast hull instead of a riveted one, but was otherwise identical to the M3. Later production models had no side doors or floor escape hatch. Note that the tank is fitted with the M2 gun and thus ▮ to have a large counterweight on the ▮ end of the gun barrel.

SPECIFICATIONS	M3 – Lee I	M3 – Grant I	M3A5 – Grant II
Crew	7	6	7
Battle weight	61,500 lb	62,000 lb	64,000 lb
Length	18 ft 6 in	18 ft 6 in	18 ft 6 in
Width	8 ft 11 in	8 ft 11 in	8 ft 11 in
Height	10 ft 3 in	9 ft 11 in	10 ft 3 in
Armour, max/min	2 in/$\frac{1}{2}$ in	2 in/$\frac{1}{2}$ in	2 in/$\frac{1}{2}$ in
Engine	9-cylinder Wright (Continental) R975 EC2	9-cylinder Wright (Continental) R975 EC2	12-cylinder General Motors 6046
Armament:			
primary	75 mm gun M2 or M3 37 mm gun M5 or M6	75 mm gun M2 37 mm gun M5 or M6	75 mm gun M2 or M3 37 mm gun M5 or M6
secondary	One .30 coax with 37 mm One .30 in turret cupola One .30 in front plate (two in early models)	One .30 coax with 37 mm Two .30 in front plate (one in later models) One .30 flexible AA (optional) One 2-in mortar (smoke) in turret	One .30 coax with 37 mm Two .30 in front plate (one in early models) One .30 flexible AA (optional)
PERFORMANCE			
Max speed	21 mph	21 mph	25 mph
Road radius	120 miles	120 miles	120 miles
Vertical obstacles	2 ft	2 ft	2 ft
Trench crossing	7 ft 6 in	7 ft 6 in	7 ft 6 in
Fording depth	3 ft 4 in	3 ft 4 in	3 ft 4 in

The M3A5 was simila▮ to the M3A3 but had ▮ riveted hull. This particular model, the M3A5E1, was fitted w▮ automatic transmiss▮ giving the tank great acceleration, driver comfort and firing p▮ stability.

The M3A2 had an all-welded hull and a cast turret. Tests showed that the new hull was stronger and offered better protection – including obviating the danger from 'popping' rivets – as well as being easier and cheaper to manufacture. Only 12 were produced at the Baldwin Locomotive Works, before production shifted to the M3A3.

An early M3A3, which was the M3 fitted with a new power plant – twin General Motors diesel engines, known as the Model 6046 engine. This tank was standardised as the M3A3, but later the designation was restricted to models with welded hulls.

The M3A4 ascending a [?] slope. This version was fitted with the Chrysler A57 Multibank petrol engine. The engine compartment had to be lengthened and raised to accommodate the new engine. Two vertical fuel tanks were lost, but this was compensated for by enlarging the sponson tanks. The longer hull also required modifications to the suspension system and longer tracks (83 tracks instead of 79).

THE M3 IN ACTION

The first M3s to see action were those sent to the British Eighth Army in the Western Desert in 1942, while they were manning the Gazala Line which extended inland from Gazala on the coast, the southernmost pivot being the Free French stronghold of Bir Hacheim. The Gazala Line comprised a deep belt of wire and minefields, interspersed with fortified localities known as Boxes, which were usually occupied in not less than brigade strength. Rommel's second major offensive in January 1942 rapidly reached the Gazala Line, but by then the DAK had virtually outrun its lines of supply. There followed a four months' stalemate, while both sides built up their strength before the Germans resumed their offensive. It was during this period that the British received tank reinforcements, including 167 Grants, together with teams of American instructors to explain all about the new tanks to the British crews.

One such British tank man was Jake Wardrop of the 5th Royal Tank Regiment, and his thoughts about the new tanks are quite clear and unequivocal: 'The new tanks were arriving now and they were super, the finest things we had ever seen. They had a nine-cylinder radial engine, were quite fast and had a crew of six, Commander, gunner and operator in the top turret, and driver, gunner and loader down below. The gun was 37 mm and the bottom one a 75 mm . . .' The new tanks were allocated to the 1st and 7th Armoured Divisions, most of them going to 4th Armoured Brigade of the latter division, in the ratio of two Grant squadrons to one Stuart squadron in each armoured regiment.

The new tanks proved their worth during the subsequent German attack, Rommel even making a special note in his diary that a new American tank had '. . . torn great holes in our ranks', while these desert battles also gave some American tank crews their first taste of combat. Three tank crews, under Major Henry C. Lodge, were attached to the 1st Royal Tank Regiment when early in June 1942 they took part in the heavy fighting around Knightsbridge and Acroma, knocking out some nine enemy tanks. After the battle they were sent home to pass on their valuable battle experience.

Of the 167 Grants sent over from USA, nearly half were destroyed, mostly by the dreaded 88 mm German gun, during the

An early Grant being demonstrated to British troops in North Africa.

General Lees, belonging to the Fort Garry Horse of Canada, on training 'somewhere in England'.

'Gazala Gallop', but more continued to arrive in Egypt, so that by the time of the now historic Battle of El Alamein, in October 1942, there were 210 Grants in the Eighth Army, together with 270 M4 Shermans.

FIRST AMERICAN ACTION

The M3 was the first medium tank to be used by the Armored Force on training manoeuvres in any quantities, being widely employed on this role in 1941 and 1942.

It was normal for units going overseas to change their M3s for M4s, but one armored division did not do so, the 1st Armored Division. When 'The Old Ironsides' landed in Northern Ireland in May 1942, the medium battalions of their armored regiments had M3s. Again, when they landed near Oran in North Africa, as part of the centre task force of Operation TORCH, one medium tank battalion of M3s was included. Although many of the battle casualties of 1st Armored Division were

replaced with Shermans, some M3s fought on throughout the campaign, and at the end of hostilities in North Africa there were still 51 M3s on the divisional strength. These were later handed over to the French for driver training.

The M3 was not used again in action as a gun tank by the American forces in either the Mediterranean or European theatres, although it did see action in the Pacific in late 1943. The 193rd Tank Battalion had M3s when they supported the 27th Infantry Division in the capture of the Gilbert Islands in November 1943. The British XIVth Army in Burma had both Lees and Grants in small numbers, continuing to use them throughout their successful campaign against the Japanese, long after the tank had officially been declared obsolete (April 1944). Over 1,300 M3 tanks were also given to the Russians under the lend-lease programme and saw action against German armour.

tank crew belonging 1st Armored Division laxes during training Ireland prior to going t to North Africa. te the 'pup' tents, ms of brew kit, etc, is the 75 mm gun ield balanced on top the turret.

A small number of M3s were used in Burma by the British XIVth Army. Here three Grants cross a stream on the way into action on the Imphal front.

Little information is available on the employment of the large number of M3s which served in Russia. Here a Lee 'brews' during an action on the steppes.

CANADIAN MEDIUM TANKS
RAM I AND RAM II

The British Tank Mission, in collaboration with the Canadian General Staff, designed a modified M3 for production in Canada by the Montreal Locomotive Works, which was called the Ram. The Ram used the standard M3 mechanical components, with a Canadian-designed hull and cast turret. The first 50 vehicles mounted a 2-pdr gun and were designated Mk I, the remainder, the Mk II, were armed with a 6-pdr. 1,899 Ram IIs had been built by the summer of 1943. The Ram was only ever used for training in Canada and the UK, although many were later converted for special usage and saw action, the most notable being as an armoured personnel carrier – Ram Kangaroo, which carried 11 men and a crew of two.

The Ram chassis was also used as the basis of a self-propelled gun, the Sexton, which mounted a 25-pdr field howitzer, and for numerous other variants including an ammunition carrier – Wallaby, an ARV Mk I and Mk II, AVRE, 3.7-in AA gun mount, flame thrower and searchlight.

The Canadian-built Ram I medium tank, which used basic M3 mechanical components, but with a British/Canadian designed hull and turret. The pilot model is seen here at APG in August 1941. It mounted a 2-pdr gun.

Sexton 25-pdr self-propelled guns being loaded at a base on the south coast of England, circa October 1944. The Sexton was the British version of the M7 Priest, and it mounted the standard 25-pdr howitzer on a Ram chassis. Produced by the Montreal Locomotive Works, some 2,150 were built between 1943 and 1945.

Driver's position in the Ram I.

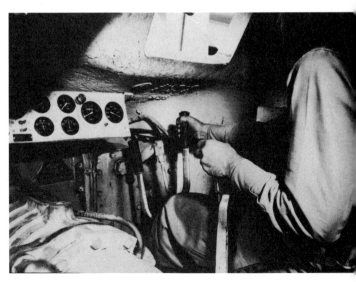

VARIANTS

Many AFVs used the basic M3 chassis or components. The SP artillery variants are described later, but here is a selection of the rest:

Tank Recovery Vehicle M31. This was a standard M3, with its guns removed (often replaced with dummy barrels) and a rear-mounted boom and winch added for recovery work. The winch had a 60,000 lb pull. M31B1 was the same conversion on the M3A3 and the M31B2 on the M3A5.

Fully Tracked Prime Mover M33. Starting in December 1943, the Chester Tank Depot converted 133 M31 tank recovery vehicles into prime movers, by removing the turret, boom, winch, etc. A high pressure compressor was added to provide braking for the gun being towed (8-inch gun or 240 mm howitzer). The conversions were necessary due to delays in production of the M6 high speed tractor.

Mine Exploder T1. First of the roller type of mechanical mine exploders, the T1, fitted in front of the M3 tank, was not very successful.

Flame Gun E3. The E3 flame thrower replaced the 37 mm in the turret of the M3; it was only used for trials.

Shop Tractor T10. This was the US version of the British-designed Canal Defence Light (see later).

Miscellaneous. Other US variants which never went into service included: 3-inch Gun Motor Carriage T24, 3-inch Gun Motor Carriage T40, 40 mm Gun Motor Carriage T36 and Heavy Tractor T16.

BRITISH AND COMMONWEALTH VARIANTS

Grant ARV. British conversion of both the Grant I and II, with guns removed and a towing winch and 'A' frame hoist added. (American M31 TRV was known as the Grant ARV I.)

Grant Scorpion III and IV. A flail-type of minefield clearing device was fitted (the 75 mm gun had to be removed to clear flails and a counterweight added to the rear). The flail rotor was driven by a separate small motor at the rear (Scorpion IV had two flail motors instead of just one).

Grant CDL. This 'secret weapon' had the rotating turret removed and replaced by an armoured searchlight housing covering a 13 million candlepower carbon arc light, which

M3 Lee with the E3 flame gun fitted in place of the 37 mm. Note also that the 75 mm gun has been removed for these trials.

A CDL on training in Wales.

Front view of the Grant Scorpion IV flail mine clearing tank.

shone through a slit (2ft × 2in) with an armoured shutter. A complete tank brigade was equipped to provide artificial moonlight for the Rhine and Elbe crossings in 1945.

Grant Command. Additional radio equipment and map tables, etc, fitted so that it could be used as a command vehicle. Sometimes its guns were removed and replaced with external wooden dummies.

Grant ARV Mk II. An Australian conversion of the standard Grant for recovery purposes.

TOTAL BUILT

A total of 6,258 M3 medium tanks were built between April 1941 and November 1942. They were built by five different manufacturers.

M3 TANK PRODUCTION					
Detroit Tank Arsenal			**American Locomotive Company**		
M3	–	3,243	M3	–	385
M3A4	–	109	M3A1	–	300
		3,352			685
Baldwin Locomotive Works			**Pressed Steel Car Company**		
M3	–	295	M3	–	501
M3A2	–	12			501
M3A3	–	322			
M3A5	–	591	**Pullman Standard Manufacturing**		
		1,220	**Company**		
			M3	–	500	500
				Grand total:	6,258

T6

About the same time as production was first authorised for the M3, the Ordnance Committee directed that work should begin on its successor, as they realised only too well that the M3 would never be anything other than a stop-gap. In designing the new medium tank, emphasis was to be put on correcting the major drawbacks of the hasty M3 design, but at the same time as much of the old as possible would be retained, so that the new tank could go into production with the minimum loss of time and effort on the assembly lines. The Armored Force submitted their detailed requirements in late August 1940, but the design team had first to finish its work on the M3 before starting on the new project, so it was New Year before they really got down to detailed planning. Sensibly they decided to use the same proven basic chassis, lower hull, suspension, transmission and engine as the M3. The major changes they proposed were to the upper hull, in the centre of which was to be a large cast, fully traversing turret. Main armament would be the improved 75 mm gun, with a coaxial .30-calibre machine-gun, thus eliminating the 37 mm entirely. The crew was reduced to five men, three in the turret (commander, gunner and loader/radio operator) and two in the hull (driver and co-driver/hull gunner). The Amer-

icans had thus adopted the British arrangement of mounting the radio in the turret rather than in the hull, saving a sixth crew member and permitting the tank to be crewed, in an emergency, by only four men.

It is interesting to speculate on just how much influence the British had on the design of the T6. A hitherto unpublished account of the work of the British Purchasing/British Supply Mission (held in the Tank Museum Library) postulates that perhaps many of the ideas put into the Sherman may have originated from the Ram, which of course it closely resembles, viz: 'In order to induce the US Ordnance to accept the basic changes in design incorporated in the Ram, General Pratt in March 1941 arranged a visit by Colonel J. B. Christmas of the US Ordnance to the Montreal Locomotive Works to view the Ram mock-up. About two months later, the British were in their turn invited to inspect the new American tank, called the General Sherman, which revealed a striking resemblance to the Ram tank! It is difficult to avoid the conclusion that the early appearance of the improved American tank is directly attributable to the efforts made by the British to demonstrate their ideas through the medium of the Ram tank. The alternative view can only be that the Ram tank either inspired or crystallized the ideas of the Americans which

Below. Front view of the medium tank T6 pilot model, photographed at APG on 16 September 1941. The gun was the M2 75 mm and was linked to a special sight rotor on the top front of the turret for use by the gunner. Double counterweights were needed as the gun mount was designed for the longer barrelled 75 mm gun (M3), so it was badly out of balance.

Below right. Front view of the wooden mockup of the medium tank T6, which was authorised to be built at APG in May 1941.

MODELS OF THE M4 MEDIUM TANK

Model	British name	Main characteristics	First produced	Quantity
M4	Sherman 1 (late production with cast upper front hull: Sherman Hybrid 1)	Welded hull: Continental R-975 petrol engine. Early vehicles had three-piece bolted nose and narrow M34 gun mount: very late vehicles had combination cast/rolled hull front.	July 1942	6,748
M4A1	Sherman 2	As for M4, but with a cast hull. First model into full production. Early vehicle has M3 type bogie units, M2 75 mm gun and counterweights, twin fixed machine-guns in hull front (later eliminated and M3 75 mm introduced). Nose altered from three-piece bolted to one-piece cast. M34A1 gun mount and sand shields added later.	Feb 1942	6,281
M4A2	Sherman 3	As for M4 but never had cast/rolled hull. General Motors 6046 diesel engine due to shortage of petrol engines.	April 1942	8,053
M4A3	Sherman 4	Welded hull and one-piece cast nose: 500 hp Ford GAA V-8 petrol engine. Most advanced of series with 75 mm gun. Mainly retained for US Army use.	May 1942	1,690
M4A4	Sherman 5	Welded hull and three-piece bolted nose. Chrysler A 57 Multibank 370 hp petrol engine, requiring hull to be lengthened to 19ft 10½ in, but increasing speed to 25 mph.	July 1942	7,499
M4A6	—	Final basic model with M4A4 hull and chassis and 450 hp RD-1820 Caterpillar radial diesel engine. Cast/rolled front.	Oct 1943	75
			Sub-total	30,346
M4(105)	—	Mounted the close-support 105 mm Howitzer M4 in an M52 mount in the turret.	Feb 1944	1,641
M4A1(76)W	—	Mounted the 76 mm gun instead of 75 mm. The 'W'	Jan 1944	3,426
M4A2(76)W	—	stands for 'Wet Stowage' – the ammunition was stowed	May 1944	2,915
M4A3(75)W	—	in water-protected racks below the turret instead of in	Feb 1944	3,071
M4A3(76)W	—	the sponsons, eg, ten boxes on the hull floor held 100 × 75 mm rounds and needed 37.1 gallons of water, with a further gallon to protect the four ready rounds. The water contained both ethylene glycol, to prevent freezing, and a corrosion inhibiter, known as 'Ammudamp'.	March 1944	4,542
M4A3(105)	—	CS Howitzer for M4(105 mm).	May 1944	3,039
Assault Tank M4A3E2	—	Heavily armoured version (thicker armour put weight up to 84,000 lb), including a more heavily armoured turret, seven inches on gun shield. Tracks had permanent grousers fitted to improve the ride. Nicknamed 'Jumbo'.	June 1944	254
			Sub-total	18,888
			Total	49,234

culminated in the famous Sherman tank (M4).'[9]

A number of changes were made after a wooden mockup of the T6 had been examined, which included the removal of the commander's cupola, thus reducing the overall height by nearly a foot although the tank was still tall by comparison with its battlefield contemporaries. Approval was then given for a pilot model to be build at APG, using a cast upper hull. At the same time Rock Island Arsenal was ordered to build a second pilot with a welded upper hull. The APG pilot was complete by early September 1941 and as the photographs show, it had sponson doors on either side of the hull. Main armament was a 75 mm gun M2 model but, as the mounting had been designed for the newer, longer-barrelled M3 gun, it was badly out of balance and had to be fitted with a double counter-weight on the end of the barrel. Following discussions with the Armored Force, Ordnance carried out various modifications, the most obvious being the removal of the sponson doors, which materially strengthened the armoured protection of the hull and simplified casting. The new tank was standardised on 5 September 1941, as the medium tank M4, and the construction of production pilots began two months later. There were now, therefore, already two versions of the Sherman, the one with a welded upper hull being designated the M4, while the one with the cast upper hull was designated the M4A1. The British called the

75 mm gun mount en from above in the turret.

NOTES
1. The Canadians also built the Sherman M4A1, which they called the Grizzly I. It was essentially identical to the US version except for having British stowage, British radio (WS 19), a two-inch bomb thrower and Canadian CDP tracks. Only 188 were built. A variation was the AA Skink which mounted quad 20 mm Polsten.
2. The missing M4A5 designation was for the Canadian-built Ram.
3. When the Horizontal Volute Spring Suspension (HVSS) and 23-inch tracks were introduced later in the war, the suffix 'Y' was added to the British designation of the Shermans so equipped. The Americans nicknamed any Sherman equipped with HVSS as an 'Easy Eight', after the E8 designation given to the HVSS trials tanks.
4. The British also used the following nomenclature for various types of armament: 75 mm gun – Sherman; 76 mm gun – Sherman A; 105 mm howitzer – Sherman B; 17-pdr gun – Sherman C.
5. A major rework of many of the early production models took place in 1944. This included a complete overhaul, new tracks, new wiring, fitting of appliqué armour, etc.

M4 the Sherman 1, and the M4A1 the Sherman 2.

FIRST PRODUCTION

The first Sherman to be produced in quantity was the M4A1 model which appeared in February 1942, production starting at the Lima Locomotive Works, where an assembly line had been established to fill British orders. The very first M4A1 off the assembly line actually used a T6 upper hull casting, with the holes for the side doors welded up. It was immediately taken over by Ordnance for test purposes and never left the USA. The second tank to be built was shipped to England, bearing the name MICHAEL on its side (see photograph), in

Michael, the second production M4A1 produced at the Lima Locomotive Works, see here on the Horse Guards Parade in the centre of London. It was so named in honour of Michael Dewar, head of the British Tank Mission.

SHERMAN – EXAMPLE DATA (MAIN MODELS)

MODEL	M4 (mid-production)	M4A1 (early production)	M4A2 (late production)	M4A3 (mid-production)	M4A4 (early production)	M4A6 (late production)
Crew	5	5	5	5	5	5
Weight (combat loaded)	66,900 lb	66,800 lb	70,200 lb	66,700 lb	69,700 lb	78,000 lb
Length	19 ft 4 in	19 ft 2 in	19 ft 5 in	19 ft 4½ in	19 ft 10½ in	19 ft 10½ in
Width	8 ft 7 in	8 ft 7 in	8 ft 7 in	8 ft 7 in	8 ft 7 in	8 ft 7 in
Height (over turret hatch)	9 ft	9 ft	9 ft	9 ft	9 ft	9 ft
Ground clearance	17 in	17 in	17 in	17 in	15¾ in	15¾ in
Tread (centre to centre of tracks)	83 in	83 in	83 in	83 in	83 in	83 in
Ground pressure	13.7 psi	13.7 psi	14.4 psi	13.7 psi	13.2 psi	13.2 psi
Ground contact length	147 in	147 in	147 in	147 in	160 in	160 in
PERFORMANCE						
Max, road speed	24 mph	24 mph	30 mph	26 mph	25 mph	30 mph
Gradient	60%	60%	60%	60%	60%	60%
Trench crossing	7 ft 5 in	7 ft 5 in	7 ft 5 in	7 ft 5 in	8 ft	8 ft
Vertical obstacle	2 ft	2 ft	2 ft	2 ft	2 ft	2 ft
Fording depth	3 ft 6 in	3 ft 6in	3 ft 6in	3 ft 6 in	3 ft 6 in	3 ft 6 in
Fuel capacity	175 gal petrol	175 gal petrol	148 gal diesel	168 gal petrol	160 gal petrol	138 gal diesel
Cruising range (on roads)	120 miles	120 miles	150 miles	130 miles	100 miles	120 miles
ENGINE						
Make	Continental	Continental	General Motors	Ford	Chrysler	Caterpillar
Model	R957C1 Petrol	R957C1 Petrol	6046 diesel	GAA Petrol	A 57 Petrol	RD-1820 Petrol
Type	9-cylinder 4-cycle radial	9-cylinder 4-cycle radial	12-cylinder 2-cycle twin in-line	8-cylinder 4-cycle, 60° Vee	30-cylinder 4-cyle Multibank	9-cylinder 4-cycle radial
Net hp at rpm	350 at 2,400	350 at 2,400	375 at 2,100	450 at 2,600	370 at 2,850	450 at 2,000

honour of Mr Michael Dewar, head of the British Tank Mission. This particular Sherman has been preserved at the Tank Museum, Bovington Camp, Dorset. A month after Lima started their production, M4A1s began to be produced by the Pressed Steel Car Company, and in May 1942 the Pacific Car and Foundry

Company also commenced their production run. All three factories continued production until 1943, the last M4A1 being built in December 1943, by which time a total of 6,281 had been constructed. Production of the welded hull M4 began at the Pressed Steel Car Company in July 1942, the angular shaped hull

BREAKDOWN OF SHERMAN GUN TANK PRODUCTION

Factory (Model, numbers produced and dates)	Total		
American Locomotive Company		M4A3E2 – 254 (May – Jul 1944)	
M4 – 2,150 (Jan – Dec 1943)		M4A3(76)W – 525 (Oct – Dec 1944)	11,358
M4A2 – 150 (Sept 1942 – Apr 1943)	2,300		
		Ford Motor Company	
		M4A3 – 1,690 (Jun 1943 – Sept 1944)	1,690
Baldwin Locomotive Works			
M4 – 1,233 (Jan – Dec 1943)		**Lima Locomotive Works**	
M4A2 – 12 (Oct – Nov 1943)	1,245	M4A1 – 1,655 (Feb 1942 – Sept 1943)	1,655
Chrysler Detroit Tank Arsenal		**Pacific Car and Foundry Company**	
M4 – 1,676 (Aug 1943 – Jan 1944)		M4A1 – 926 (May 1942 – Dec 1943)	926
M4(105) – 1,641 (Feb 1943 – Mar 1945)			
M4A3(76)W – 4,017 (Mar 1944 – Apr 1945)		**Pressed Steel Car Company**	
M4A3(105) – 3,039 (Jun 1944 – Jun 1945)		M4 – 1,000 (Jul 1942 – Aug 1943)	
M4A4 – 7,499 (Jul 1942 – Sept 1943)		M4A1 – 3,700 (Mar 1942 – Dec 1943)	
M4A6 – 75 (Oct 1943 – Feb 1944)	17,947	M4A1(76) – 3,426 (Jan 1944 – Jun 1945)	
		M4A2(76)W – 21 (May – June 1945)	8,147
Federal Machine and Welder Company			
M4A2 – 540 (Dec 1942 – Jan 1944)	540	**Pullman Standard Manufacturing Company**	
		M4 – 689 (Jun – Sept 1943)	
Fisher, Grand Blanc Arsenal		M4A2 – 2,737 (Apr 1942 – Sept 1943)	3,426
M4A2 – 4,614 (Apr 1942 – Jun 1944)			
M4A2(76)W – 2,894 (Jun 1944 – Jun 1945)			
M4A3(75)W – 3,071 (Feb 1944 – Mar 1945)		Grand total	49,234

being slightly larger than the cast version, thus giving more room for ammunition stowage (97 rounds instead of 90 on the M4A1).

So began the enormous production run of Sherman gun tanks. They would be built by many American factories, reach the staggering total of 49,234, over half of the total American wartime tank production, and far more than the entire German tank industry could build in the same period. Shermans would be used by nearly every Allied nation, in every theatre of operations and in just about every operational role one can imagine for an AFV. The tables on this page give outline details of all the basic Sherman models.

In order to meet production quotas other manufacturers were soon brought into the Sherman programme. M4 production began at Baldwin Locomotive Works in January 1943, at the American Locomotive Company in February 1943, at the Pullman Standard Car Company in May 1943, and finally at the Detroit Tank Arsenal in August 1943. When production ended in January 1944, 6,748 M4s, equipped with the 75 mm gun, had been produced. The later production models at the Detroit Tank Arsenal had a combination cast/rolled hull front, the upper part being made of a single steel casting which extended behind the driver's and co-driver's hatches, and was welded to the rest of the rolled homogeneous plate hull. As the table shows, later on more M4s, equipped with 105 mm howitzers, and more M4A1s, equipped with 76 mm guns, were built. (Details of these AFVs are given later).

The Pacific Car and
Foundry Company
produced this pilot
model of the M4A1, wi
its cast hull. Note that
the early gunner's
sighting device has bee
replaced by a periscop
sight in the turret roof

GENERAL DESCRIPTION[10]

'These medium tanks (M4 and M4A1) are armored, track-laying vehicles designed to give greater protection to the crew and more effective firing power than previous model medium tanks. The thickness of the front section of the hull varies from $1\frac{1}{2}$ inches to 3 inches. The M4 has a welded hull; the M4A1 has a cast hull; both have cast turrets. Both turret and hull are so curved as to present little opportunity for a direct hit on a flat surface from any angle. This tank provides the tactical advantage of a lower silhouette than previous medium tanks. This also results in a lowered centre of gravity, making it more difficult for the tank to tip over. The principal armament is the 75 mm gun mounted in the rotating turret. A cal .30 gun is mounted together with the 75 mm gun and both move as a unit. With a 360° traverse and greater elevation and de-

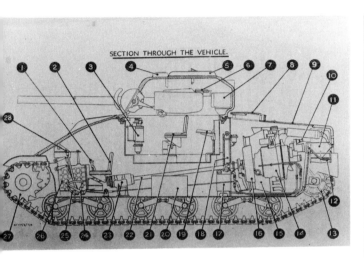

Section taken through an M4 (extracted from the Technical Manual) (Tank Museum).

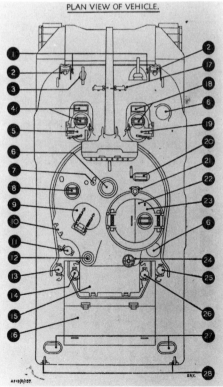

Plan view of the Sherman – late model M4/M4A1 (Tank Museum).

Section Through the Vehicle	
1 Gear lever	14 Engine
2 Driver's seat	15 Fan shroud
3 Main armament stabilizer	16 Clutch
4 Turret ventilator	17 Engine oil canister
5 Rotating cupola	18 Engine oil cooler
6 Commander's seat (upper)	19 Commander's seat (lower)
7 Wireless set	20 Battery box
8 Clutch compartment cover	21 Turret gunner's seat
9 Engine compartment cover	22 Propeller shaft
	23 Dynamo
10 Cranking handle socket	24 Clutch pedal
	25 Accelerator pedal
11 Air cleaner	26 Gearbox
12 Air exhaust deflector	27 Sprocket
13 Track-adjusting wheel	28 Steering levers

Plan View of the Vehicle	
1 Headlamp socket plug	16 Top engine cover
2 Combined head and side lamp	17 Gun travelling lock
	18 Hull gunner's periscopes
3 Siren	19 Hull gunner's hatch
4 Driver's periscopes	20 Turret gunner's periscope
5 Driver's hatch	
6 Ventilator	21 AA mounting bracket
7 Spotlight socket	22 Rotating cupola
8 Operator's periscope	23 Crew commander's hatch
9 Operator's hatch	
10 Pistol port	24 'B' set aerial mounting
11 Auxiliary generator fuel tank filler cover	25 Right hand horizontal fuel tank filler cover
12 'A' set aerial mounting	26 Right hand vertical fuel tank filler cover
13 Left hand horizontal fuel tank filler cover	
14 Left hand vertical fuel tank filler cover	27 Fuel tank air inlet louvres
15 Clutch compartment cover	28 Tail lamps

Underneath of the Sherman M4/M4A1 (Tank Museum).

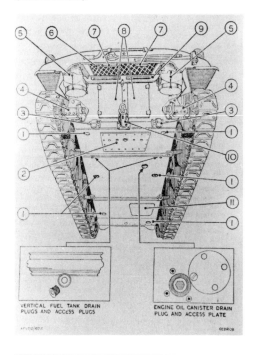

VERTICAL FUEL TANK DRAIN PLUGS AND ACCESS PLUGS

ENGINE OIL CANISTER DRAIN PLUG AND ACCESS PLATE

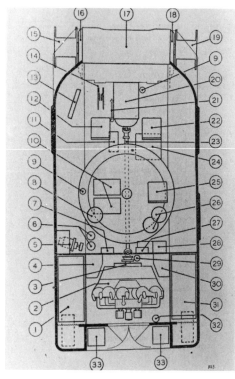

Sherman M4/M4A1, layout of main components (Tank Museum).

Underside of the Vehicle	
1 Hull drain valves	7 Engine exhaust pipes
2 Engine inspection plate	8 Engine rear doors
3 Towing shackles	9 Air exhaust deflector
4 Track adjusting assembly	10 Light equipment towing hook
5 Air cleaner	11 Emergency escape hatch
6 Auxiliary generator exhaust pipe	

Layout of Main Components	
1 Left hand horizontal fuel tank	17 Differential
2 Engine	18 Right hand final drive
3 Clutch and fan	19 Right hand driving sprocket
4 Left hand vertical fuel tank	20 Gearbox
5 Auxiliary generator and fuel tank	21 Gear lever
6 Fixed fire extinguishers	22 Hull gunner's seat
7 Transmission oil cooler	23 Propeller shaft
8 Operator's seat	24 Escape hatch
9 Portable fire extinguisher	25 Turret gunner's seat
10 Batteries	26 Commander's seat (upper and lower)
11 Dynamo	27 Engine oil cooler
12 Driver's seat	28 Engine oil canister
13 Instrument panel	29 Fuel filter
14 Steering levers	30 Right hand vertical fuel tank
15 Left hand driving sprocket	31 Right hand horizontal fuel tank
16 Left hand final drive	32 Engine oil filter
	33 Air cleaner

pression (from $+25°$ to $-12°$) than was possible with the gun mounted on the side of the tank, as in the Medium Tank M3, the range of the 75 mm gun is greatly increased and its firepower made effective in any direction. Other armament in the tank includes a cal .30 MG in a flexible mount located in the right bow of the tank and a cal .50 anti-aircraft gun to be used in a bracket mount on top of the revolving hatch of the turret. A clip is mounted in the top rear of the turret to carry a cal .45 submachine-gun which can be used through the pistol port located in the left rear side of the turret.

'The tank crew consists of five men. The driver sits at the left bow of the tank, to the left of the transmission. The assistant driver's

46

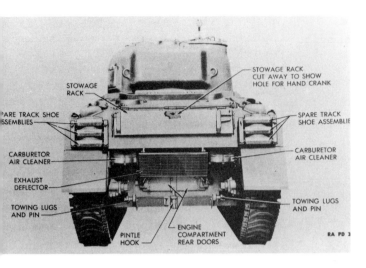

STOWAGE RACK
CUT AWAY TO SHOW
HOLE FOR HAND CRANK

STOWAGE
RACK

SPARE TRACK SHOE
ASSEMBLIES

SPARE TRACK
SHOE ASSEMBLIE

CARBURETOR
AIR CLEANER

CARBURETOR
AIR CLEANER

EXHAUST
DEFLECTOR

TOWING LUGS
AND PIN

TOWING LUGS
AND PIN

PINTLE
HOOK

ENGINE
COMPARTMENT
REAR DOORS

RA PD 3

Rear view of M4/M4A1 (Tank Museum).

Driver's controls a medium tank M4/M4A1 (Tank Museum).

Driver's Controls, Medium Tank M4 and M4A1

1 Instrument panel	6 Hand throttle
2 Starting switches	7 Siren switch
3 Compass	8 Clutch pedal
4 Breather	9 Accelerator pedal
5 Steering levers	10 Gear shift lever

position is in the right bow, to the right of the transmission and directly behind the cal .30 MG. The tank commander is stationed at the rear of the turret, just to the right of the shoulder guard of the 75 mm gun and almost directly behind the gunner. The 75 mm gunner's station is in the right front just ahead of the tank commander. The loader's[11] station is to the left of the gun. Access to the tank is provided through the two hatches in the bow and the revolving hatch in the turret.[12] For use in an emergency an escape hatch is provided in the tank floor, directly back of the assistant driver's seat. When all hatches are closed, indirect vision is provided for each member of the crew by means of periscopes. With the exception of the gunner's periscope these vision devices are mounted so that they can be tilted up or down and rotated through a 360° traverse. The gunner's periscope is synchronised with the gun, contains a telescope sight and changes its line of sight only if the gun is elevated or depressed or the turret rotated. For emergency use, the driver and assistant driver are provided with direct vision through a narrow slit in the direction vision guard in the front armor plate. Two additional M6 periscopes will replace these slits in later production models.

'The tank is powered by a 400 horsepower, nominal 9-cylinder radial aircraft type engine.[13] Access to the engine is provided through a hinged engine compartment top plate, the rear engine doors, and the inspection plate located beneath the engine. Horizontal mufflers, running from front to rear under the engine compartment top plates, reduce engine noise considerably below that of previous model medium tanks. The air cleaners are mounted at the rear and outside the engine compartment for easier servicing. An air inlet cover in the front engine compartment top plate gives access to the fan compartment. The tank has four fuel tanks, two vertical tanks, and two large sponson tanks, located at the right and left front of the engine compartment. They are filled through four caps located on the top of the hull to the right and left rear of the turret. An auxiliary generator set[14] is located in the left rear of the fighting compartment. Its purpose is to provide an additional source of electrical power and also to provide heat for the engine compartment in cold weather. The tank is equipped with radio for inter-tank communications and with an interphone system for

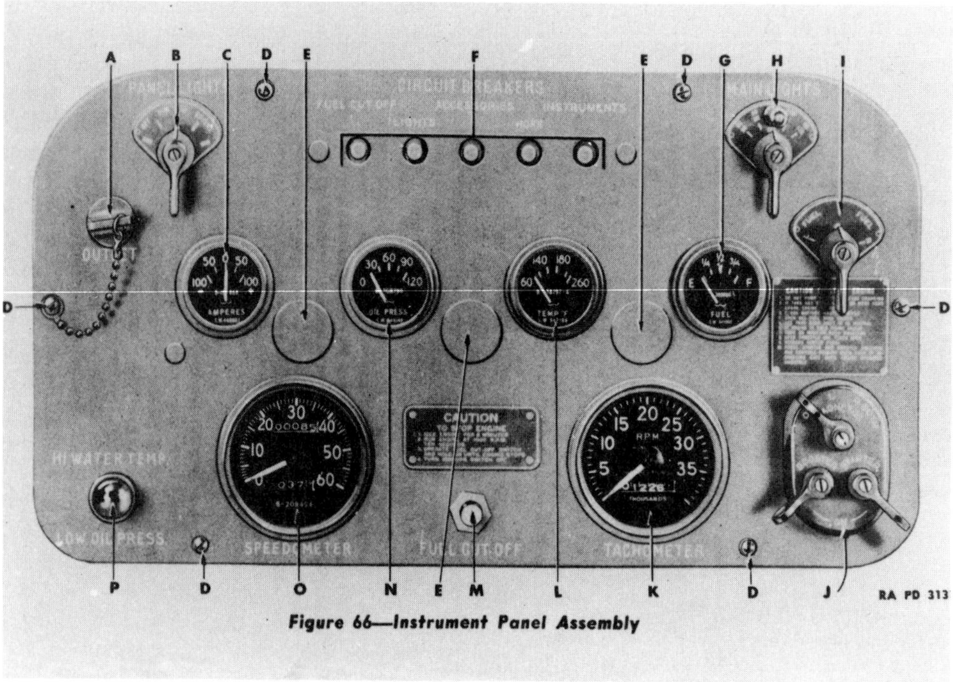

Instrument panel assembly, driver's station M4 (105 mm howitzer) and M4A1 (76 mm gun) (Tank Museum).

Figure 66—Instrument Panel Assembly

Instrument Panel Assembly, M4 and M4A1

A	Utility outlet socket	G	Fuel gauge	L	Engine oil
B	Panel light switch	H	Main light switch		temperature gauge
C	Ammeter	I	Fuel gauge selector	M	Fuel cut-off switch
D	Panel attaching		switch	N	Oil pressure gauge
	screw	J	Cranking motor and	O	Speedometer
E	Panel light cover		magneto switch	P	Low oil pressure
F	Circuit breakers	K	Tachometer		warning light

communication between the tank commander and members of the crew.'

DRIVING POSITION AND CONTROLS

The driver sat on the left side of the fighting compartment, directly under the left front hatch, which had a lid which opened upwards and outwards towards the side of the tank. His seat could be adjusted for height and moved forwards or backwards to the most comfortable driving position. His instrument panel was located to his left, at the front of the left sponson. Panel instruments (in early models) were: fuel gauge, speedometer, engine hour meter[15], tachometer, engine oil temperature gauge, oil pressure gauge, transmission oil temperature gauge, ammeter, voltmeter, ignition and starter switches, light switches, fuel cutoff switches, oil dilution switch, clock and a series of circuit breaker reset buttons for the principal circuits. A bracket-mounted com-

pass was located on the left in front of the driver.

The driver's main controls were: two steering levers with rubber grips, mounted on the floor directly ahead of his seat; a foot accelerator pedal to the right of the steering levers convenient to the driver's right foot; a hand-operated throttle mounted on the final drive housing and to the right of the steering levers; and a parking brake lever on the right side of the driver at the back of the transmission (this was a parking brake only). As with the M3, to slow down or stop the tank, the driver pulled back on both steering levers simultaneously. There was a clutch pedal to the left of the steering levers, convenient to the driver's left foot; a gearshift hand lever, located on the transmission to the right of the driver (five forward gears, neutral and reverse, with a latch to prevent accidental shifting from first gear into reverse); and a siren control, a

Gunner's controls for the 75 mm on Sherman — M4/M4A1 (Tank Museum).

MAIN ARMAMENT

The main armament of the M4 and M4A1 was the 75 mm gun M3 in the mount M34 (later models had the M34A1 mount). It was a quick-firing semi-automatic weapon, loaded by hand and when it was fired recoiled approximately one foot under the control of a hydraulic buffer system. After recoil, recuperator springs returned the gun to the firing position. During the run-out of the gun, the empty case was ejected and the breech stayed open ready for another round to be loaded. Traverse was either manual or power-assisted; using the latter the turret could be traversed through 360° in 15 seconds. Elevation was manual and there was a gyrostabilisation system operating in elevation only. Maximum firing rate was 20 rounds per minute. For the main armament 97 rounds were carried (only 90 in the M4A1), normally a mixture of types, a typical mix being 35% AP, 55% HE and 10% Smoke, but this of course varied with the tactical situation. Types of ammunition included APC M61, HE M48 and Smoke HC B1 M89. The effective ranges of these types of ammunition were approximately 1,200–1500 yards for AP, 12,000 yards for HE and 2,000 yards for Smoke. Penetration performance of the AP round naturally varied with range, type of armour attacked and angle of obliquity, but to give an example:

Type of armour attacked at 30° obliquity	APC M61 round – penetration in inches at ranges shown in yards			
	500	1,000	1,500	2,000
Homogeneous	2.6	2.4	2.2	2.0
Face hardened	2.9	2.6	2.4	2.1

GUNNER'S CONTROLS

The gunner operated the elevating and traversing controls, the stabiliser controls and the firing switches for both the 75 mm gun and the coaxial MG. These foot firing switches were brought into operation when a toggle switch on the turret switch box was pushed to the left (the 'ON' position). A red signal light then came on to warn that the foot switches were ready to operate, the right-hand one being for the 75 mm, the left-hand one for the MG. If

foot-operated button on a plate to the right and just above the clutch pedal, within easy reach of the driver's left foot. Finally there were two stop light switches, connected to the steering brake arms, which activated the stop lights only when both steering levers were pulled back simultaneously.

DRIVER'S HOOD

Although when under fire in battle, the driver normally drove closed down, the vast majority of driving was done with the driver head-up in the open hatch. It was therefore essential to have some kind of hood to protect him (and the inside of his compartment) from the weather. The hood needed a built-in windscreen, with a wiper and defroster, yet had to be capable of being folded so that it could be taken inside the tank when the hatch was closed. The final approved model had a safety glass windscreen, folding canvas top, rear and sides. When not in use it was kept folded up between the driver and the co-driver.

Interior of Turret to Show Stations

1 **Holder for hand fire** **extinguisher**	3 **Breech ring**	6 **Shoulder guard**
	4 **Commander's seat**	7 **Gunner's seat**
2 **Loader's seat**	5 **75 mm gun elevating wheel**	

they failed, then the gun could be fired manually by depressing another pedal, located directly to the left of the firing switches on the turret floor.

POWER TRAVERSE SYSTEMS

In addition to hand traverse, the turret could be turned by a power traverse system either hydraulically or electrically operated. There were three types in use in the Sherman turret, two hydraulic models made by Oilgear and Logansport, while Westinghouse made an electrical model. The best of the three was the hydraulic model made by the Oilgear Company. With the hydraulic system the turret was traversed by means of a gear mechanism operated by an oil-driven hydraulic motor. The system provided a supply of oil under pressure which was fed to one side or the other of the hydraulic motor, the direction and rate of flow, and rotation, being determined by a manually-operated control valve. When this was turned in either direction from the vertical some of the oil was fed to one of the two motor

hoses. The further the handle was turned the more oil went through the hose, thus increasing the supply to the hydraulic motor. Oil coming into the motor caused it to turn and traverse the turret in the same direction in which the handle was turned. If the control valve handle was turned in the other direction it fed oil under pressure to the other motor hose, reversing the directions of rotation and traverse of the turret. The control valve handle locked in the neutral (upright) position when the trigger was not squeezed.

With the electrical system, the turret traversing motor was supplied with 220 volts DC by the turret motor generator set. A safety switch kept the power traverse mechanism off as long as the handwheel was engaged for manual operation. Two special, two-way switches were provided, one for the gunner and the other for the commander, to enable high-speed traversing from one target to another. The traversing motor, gearbox and traversing handwheel were all located directly in front of the gunner. Another handwheel, down to the gunner's right, operated a locking clamp which, when engaged, prevented rotation of the turret, so before using power or hand traverse, it was essential that this handwheel was turned as far as possible in a clockwise direction to free the turret.

GYROSTABILISER

The Westinghouse gyrostabiliser was used to keep the gun on or very near its aimed angular position, within its free range angular movement, while the tank was moving and oscillating or pitching normally. Crews were firmly told not use the stabiliser unless the tank was in motion. To avoid draining the batteries when the tank was stationary, the gun was controlled by the hand elevating wheel, which automatically disengaged the stabiliser. Once the gun was aimed the stabiliser controlled the aimed position of the gun and the gunner only turned the handwheel when it was necessary to re-aim the gun, if the target moved, the tank changed direction or the elevation of the tank (other than that caused by normal pitching) changed.

SIGHTING ARRANGEMENTS

The initial sighting arrangement for the gunner when the Sherman first went into production was by a special sight rotor in the top front of the turret, which was linked to the gun mount. The linkage moved the top mirror of the periscope type telescopic sight to keep it in alignment with the bore of the gun. A supply of spare mirrors was carried in the tank in case the top mirror was damaged. In March 1942 it was decided to replace the rotor sight with the M4 periscope, which had a telescope built into its right side, and was installed further back on the turret roof, where it was much less vulnerable. At about the same time it was decided to fit a blade vane sight to help the commander to lay the gun quickly on to a target. The front blade was welded just to the right of the gunner's periscopic sight, the rear one attached to the turret hatch door just in front of the commander's periscope. Later these early blade vane sights were replaced with improved models, but all worked on the same principle.

SECONDARY ARMAMENT

When the M4 was first standardised, the tank had, in addition to the flexible ball-mounted MG in the right bow, two fixed .30-calibre MGs positioned to its left, which were fired by the driver (*cf* the M3). These were removed in

Telescope T92 and Telescope Mount M57 (Tank Museum).

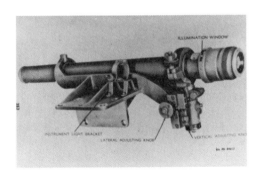

Elevation quadrant M9 (Tank Museum).

RA PD 84747

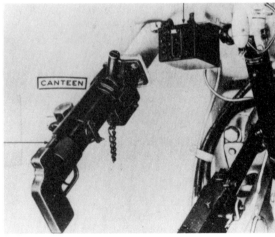

Installation of 2-inch mortar M3. The mortar is at the left. The stabilizer oil reservoir is at the top and the cylinder and piston at the bottom can be seen the .30-calibre machine gun. (Tank Museum).

Co-driver's station, showing flexible MG mounting in bow (Tank Museum).

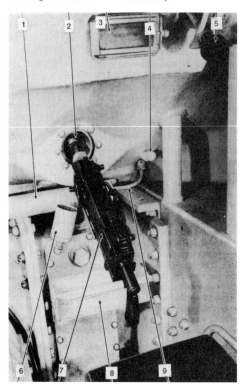

Assistant Driver's Station in Right Bow

1 **Cross shaft**	6 **Breather**
2 **Flexible mount**	7 **Cal. .30 machine gun**
3 **Direct vision**	8 **Cal. .30 ammunition**
4 **Headlamp locking pin**	**rack**
5 **Control lever for**	9 **Headlamp lead**
direct vision cover	

March 1942. Also, upon standardisation, the commander's hatch had a rotating ring around it on which was mounted a .50 AA MG (replacing the .30 MG which had been part of the commander's cupola originally fitted to the T6 mock-up). There was considerable controversy about this MG. The British in particular did not like it, and more often than not did not mount it, relying for AA protection on the special AA tanks in each squadron. In the autumn of 1942, the US Ordnance decided to replace the .50 HMG with a .30 MG but a few months later, in early 1943, had second thoughts, and the .50 was reintroduced as a standard fitment. Another weapon, which was subsequently adopted from the British, was a two-inch bomb thrower, used for providing local smoke, which was installed in the left side of the turret roof.

AMMUNITION STOWAGE

A full load of ammunition comprised:
97 rounds 75 mm on M4 (90 rounds on M4A1);
500 rounds Cal .50;
4,750 rounds Cal .30;
600 rounds Cal .45 in 30-round clips;
12 hand grenades; and
12 two-inch smoke bombs.

The main gun ammunition was stowed as follows:
8 rounds in a ready rack under the gun;
12 rounds in brackets around the lower turret basket walls;
15 rounds in a stowage rack in the left sponson;
32 rounds in two stowage racks (15 and 17) in the right sponson; and
30 rounds in the main compartment under the turret basket.

PISTOL PORT

The early production turrets of the M4 series had a pistol port in the left-hand wall, but there was a good deal of controversy as to whether or not they were useful or merely made the turret more vulnerable on that side. In February 1943 it was decided to eliminate the port and orders were issued accordingly to all factories. However, battle experience showed that the port was valuable and the order was countermanded in July 1943 so it began appearing again on tanks produced from early 1944 onwards.

ARMOUR

The type of armour used in the construction of the M4 varied both in its location on the tank and between models. For example, while both the turret of the M4 and the M4A1 were made of cast, homogeneous steel, the former had the upper of welded construction, while the latter was cast. The thickness of armour used varied according to the vulnerability of that particular part of the tank to direct enemy fire. For example, the front of the hull of the M4 was two inches thick, but the sides and rear were only $1\frac{1}{2}$ inches thick and the top just $\frac{3}{4}$ inch. The hull floor varied from an inch at the front to $\frac{1}{2}$ inch at the rear. The turret was three inches thick at the front ($3\frac{1}{2}$ inches on the gunshield), two inches on the sides and rear, and one inch on top. Armour thickness was somewhat increased on later models, but with the exception of the 'Jumbo' assault Sherman, it did not increase to any major degree.

Sloping the armour assisted in improving its ability to protect against enemy fire, but unfortunately, throughout the war the Sherman could be penetrated with ease by most contemporary enemy anti-tank and tank guns – hardly surprising when one remembers that it really had been designed to give protection against a 37 mm anti-tank weapon. It rapidly built up a reputation for being prone to catching fire, due mainly to the speed at which the ammunition propellant used ignited when struck by enemy fire. Stowing additional ammunition outside the recognised stowage bins and racks added to the hazard – but what tanker who has been in action can truthfully say that he has never been guilty of this breach of the rules? Once the ammunition had caught fire, then there was nothing the crew could do but bale out as quickly as possible. No wonder the Sherman earned the nickname of the 'Ronson Lighter' because it was virtually guaranteed to 'light every time'! As will be later explained, tank crews used a wide variety of methods to obtain further protection.

FIRE EXTINGUISHER SYSTEM

The Sherman was equipped with a fire extinguisher system consisting of two 10lb fixed and two 4lb portable carbon dioxide bottles. The fixed units were clamped to the bulkhead at the rear left of the fighting compartment, surrounding the engine. They were activated by two sets of controls, one inside near the driver's seat and one outside on the rear deck. Portable extinguishers were located on the turret basket near the loader's seat and in the left sponson near the driver.

Fixed Fire Extinguisher System, M4 and M4A1

1 Control handle cable flexible conduits
2 Cables to exterior control handles
3 Dual pull mechanism
4 Check valve to bulkhead tube
5 Cylinder assembly
6 Interior control handles
7 Remote control cable pulleys to dual pull mechanism tubes

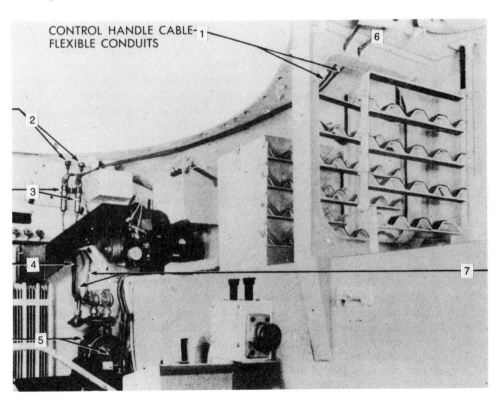

Fixed fire extinguisher system M4/M4A1 medium tanks (Tank Museum).

CONTROL HANDLE CABLE-FLEXIBLE CONDUITS

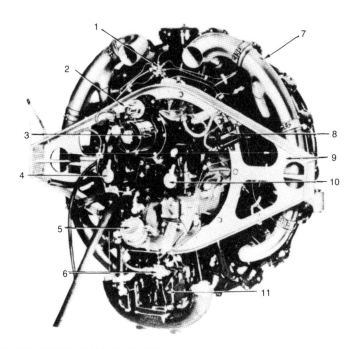

Right Rear View of Engine			
1 Priming distributor	4 Left magneto	7 Exhaust manifold	9 Engine support
2 Hand cranking	5 Fuel pump	for cylinders Nos 1, 2,	beam
attachment	6 Idle cut-off and	3 and 4	10 Right magneto
3 Cranking motor	degasser	8 Booster coil	11 Carburettor

THE MAIN ENGINE

The Wright Continental R 975 engine as fitted in the M4 and M4A1 was a nine-cylinder radial four-stroke, air-cooled petrol engine of the aircraft type. The nine cylinders were equally spaced and mounted radially on the crankcase with No 1 cylinder at the top, the remainder being numbered clockwise when viewed from the rear. The pistons were connected to a single throw crankshaft, which extended forwards through the centre of the crankcase to drive the flywheel. The timing case was secured to the crankcase and enclosed the timing gear trains and auxiliary drive gears. On this case were mounted the auxiliary components, such as starter motor, oil pumps, tachometer drive (early vehicles), magnetos, fuel pump and governor. The flywheel was mounted on the forward end of the crankshaft and was the driving member of the clutch. As the engine was designed for use in aircraft, where engine speeds were kept constant for long periods, the radial operated most efficiently under these conditions. Lubrication was by a forcefed dry sump system; cooling by a fan bolted to the clutch housing on the flywheel which drew air through an inlet louvre in the engine compartment and forced it around the cooling fins on the cylinders and out at the top of the rear hull plate. An air shroud and cowling surrounded the fan and cylinders to ensure that the air was directed at the hottest parts of the engine. The exhaust system consisted of left and right exhaust manifold assemblies that led up through elbows at the top of the exhaust manifold into two horizontally-mounted mufflers just under the engine compartment top cover. Exhaust gases were expelled through two tail pipes projecting just below the rear centre of the hull.

Four other engines would be fitted to various later models of the Sherman; two were diesels, the General Motors 6046 (fitted to the M4A2) and the RD-1820 Caterpillar (fitted to the M4A6); the other two were petrol, the Chrysler A 57 Multibank (fitted to the M4A4) and the Ford GAA V-8 (fitted to the M4A3), the one most favoured by the US Army as it was the most efficient and trouble-free.

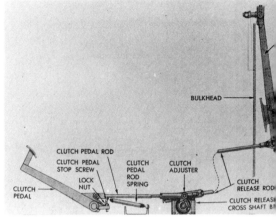

Auxiliary Generator and Controls, M4A1 (76 mm gun)	
1 Fuel tank	8 Ground strap
2 Fuel tank gauge	9 Air cleaner
3 Spark plug wire conduit	10 Heat deflector damper control
4 Regulator	11 Choke
5 Ammeter	12 Stop button
6 Circuit breaker	13 Starting rope
7 Starting button	

Side of view of the clutch controls. At the right, 1 is the clutch throwout yoke; 2 is the clutch release bearing; 3 is the clutch throwout bearing shoe; 4 is the clutch release sleeve; and 5 indicates the $\frac{1}{8}$ inch clearance when the clutch is engaged (Tank Museum).

ELECTRICAL SYSTEM AND THE AUXILIARY GENERATOR

The tank had a 24-volt DC electrical system, with a 24 V, 50 amp main generator being driven by a power take-off from the main engine. In addition, there was an auxiliary generator unit consisting of a 30 V, 1,500 Watt generator driven by a single cylinder, two-stroke, air-cooled petrol engine. The auxiliary generator (affectionately known as 'Little Joe' by most tankers) was used to charge the tank batteries (two of 12 volts wired in series) when it was not desirable to run the main engine, or when it was necessary to supplement the output of the main generator when, for example, the radio, turret traverse, gyrostabiliser, etc, imposed a heavy load upon the batteries. 'Little Joe' was mounted at the rear end of the left sponson in the fighting compartment. It had a separate fuel tank with a five-gallon capacity, sufficient to run the generator for about 12 hours.

CLUTCH, TRANSMISSION AND FINAL DRIVES

The clutch[16] was a multiple disc type, mounted inside the flywheel. It had two clutch-driven discs (one outer and one inner), one driving plate, one pressure plate and six springs assembled to the flywheel ring. Openings in the flywheel ring and flywheel allowed for air ventilation. Separator pins provided a means of separating the driven discs and driving plate. An annular release bearing was used. Power was transmitted from the clutch to the input shaft of the gearbox by a propeller shaft, which ran in a tunnel through the hull under the turret turntable to the gearbox, located at the front of the tank to the right of the driver's seat. As with the M3, it was the need for this shaft which was the major reason for the height of the tank. The propeller shaft was of one-piece construction, with a universal joint at each end. The front universal joint was connected to the shaft with a splined slip yoke.

The gearbox had five forward and one reverse gear, the second, third, fourth and fifth gears being synchronised.[17] First and reverse were in constant mesh and engaged by a sliding clutch. The final drive assembly consisted of two controlled differential steering brake assemblies and final reduction assemblies, mounted on the left and right sides of the final drive assembly. The differential was called a controlled differential because it served not only to transmit power to the final reduction units, but it also contained the brake system for

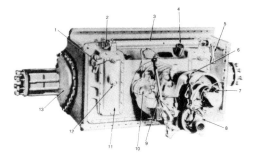

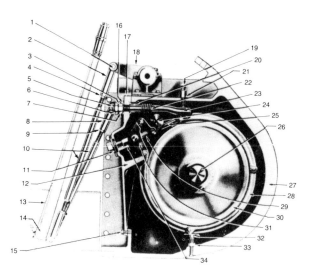

Cross section of steering brake assembly (Tank Museum).

the purpose of steering and stopping the vehicle. With this arrangement both tracks were driven when steering, so it was impossible to do a skid turn. The final reduction assembly transmitted power from the differential to the hubs of the driving sprockets. Each assembly had a set of reduction gears through which power was transmitted from the final drive shaft to the sprocket hub. Each set of final drive shaft gears was mounted on a cover bolted to the final drive housing at either end. The driving sprocket was bolted to a hub on each final reduction assembly. The double anchor steering brake was a three-shoe external contracting steering brake operating in oil. The shoe assembly and brake drum were located in each end of the final drive housing and were actuated by the steering brake control levers.

VERTICAL VOLUTE SPRING SUSPENSION

As with the M3, the Sherman was supported on six bogie suspension assemblies, bolted to the hull, three on each side. Each suspension assembly had two rubber-tyred wheels and as the tank moved across rough ground the vert-ical movement of these wheels was transferred to the supporting arms or levers, and was absorbed by two volute springs in each suspension assembly. The springs were compressed between a bracket and a lower seating or platform. This platform was pivoted in an 'H'-shaped floating lever which rested on the bogie wheel arms. The bogie wheel arms and the ends of the floating lever were fitted with detachable metal rubbing pads which prevented friction wear between the arms and the lever. As the bogie wheel rose, one end of the floating lever was forced up causing the lower spring platform to compress the springs equally. The early version of this system had guide rollers mounted on top of the bogie frames, to support the top run of track. However, by mid-1942 this type had been replaced by a new, heavy duty version employing larger volute springs, which did not leave sufficient clear-

Transmission and final drive assembly (Tank Museum).

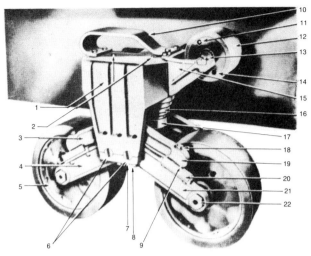

1 —
2 —
3 —
4 —
5 —
6 —
7 —
8 —
9 —
10 —
11 —
12 —
13 —
14 —
15 —
16 —
17 —
18 —
19 —
20 —
21 —
22 —

Modified type of vertical volute spring suspension. The larger springs did not allow room for the top roller above the bogie frame, so it was offset to the side (Tank Museum).

Vertical Volute Spring Suspension Assembly	
1 Volute suspension bracket	13 Support roller bracket bolt
2 Bracket plug	14 Relief valve
3 Lever	15 Support roller bracket
4 Arm	16 Volute suspension spring
5 Wheel	17 Spring seat
6 Suspension gudgeon	18 Rubbing plate retainer screw
7 Bracket cap	19 Lever
8 Bolt	20 Rubbing plate
9 Rubbing plate	21 Arm
10 Track support skid	22 Wheel gudgeon
11 Lubrication fitting	
12 Support roller	

ance for the top roller, so it was offset to the rear. The new suspension certainly reduced the number of spring failures, especially on the heavier models like the M3A4, but did nothing to improve cross-country performance on soft ground. Major improvement did not come until 1944, when the horizontal volute spring suspension (HVSS) was generally introduced.

THE TRACKS

Two individually-driven tracks propelled the tank forwards or backwards. The drive sprockets at the front pulled the tracks from the rear and laid them down in front of the advancing suspension wheels. An adjustable idler was mounted at the rear of the hull, so that the proper tension could be maintained. Each track consisted of 79[18] all-steel or steel and rubber blocks linked together to form an

endless track. Two pins passed through each block and projected at each end. The pins had rubber spacers vulcanised to them, so that when the pin was pressed into the block, the rubber formed a cushion between the pin and the steel frame. The pins of the adjoining blocks were linked by steel end connectors which were secured to the pins by bolt-type wedges. Both faces of the wedges were inclined so that when they were pulled up between the pins, they caused the adjacent pins to tilt. The angle so formed caused the track to curve closely around the rear bogie, the idler and the sprocket, thus opposing the tendency for the track to be thrown outwards by centrifugal force. There were two designs of tracks with steel and rubber blocks, three with all-steel blocks. Normal track-plate width was 16.5 inches, which was increased to 23 inches when HVSS was introduced. Other types of extended track grouser are covered in a later chapter.

COMMUNICATIONS EQUIPMENT

The M4 series were equipped with radio and interphone systems, shock-mounted, on a common base and located on a shelf in the turret bulge. Interphone boxes were provided for each member of the crew. The 12 V power supply for the system came from the vehicle batteries via a separate wiring system to the 24 V electrical system. One of the following Frequency Modulated (FM) radio telephone sets was fitted: SCR 508, SCR 528 or SCR 538, depending on the type of operation to which the tank was assigned. All had a range of between ten and twenty miles, but they were subject to terrain screening, the actual range at times being down to five miles or even less. The SCR 508 comprised a radio transmitter (model BC 604) and two radio receivers (model BC 603), mounted on a base model FT 237. It was generally used in company command tanks, so that the commander could have one set tuned to his platoon leaders and the other on the battalion net. The SCR 508 was an 80-crystal (any ten frequencies preset) push-button radio, providing voice only on 20-28 mc FM. The SCR 528 was identical except it had only one model BC 603 receiver. It was fitted in those tanks requiring two-way communic-ations, such as platoon leaders' and platoon sergeants'. Finally, the SCR 538 had no trans-mitter, just a BC 603 receiver and an inter-phone amplifier model BC 605 on the same FT 237 base mount. This set was fitted to those

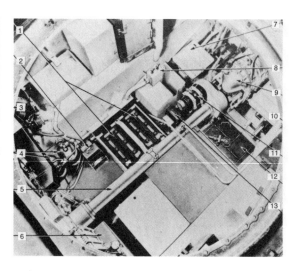

Fighting Compartment with Turret Removed

1 Batteries	7 Driver's seat
2 Auxiliary generator regulator	8 Battery switch box
	9 Transmission
3 Auxiliary generator	10 Assistant driver's seat
4 Fixed fire extinguishers	11 Generator
5 Propeller shaft housing	12 Escape door
	13 Generator regulator
6 Engine oil supply tank	

tanks which did not need to transmit although later in the war, all were issued with transmitters.

At battalion level, a second radio set was normally fitted, either an early SCR 245, or the more usual SCR 506. This was an Amplitude Modulated (AM) radio set with a rated range of 25 to 50 miles using voice and out to 100 miles using a morse key, although the earlier type of set, of course, did not have as great a range. The SCR 506 comprised a BC 653 transmitter and a BC 652 receiver, mounted on an FT 253 base. The set was located in the tank's right-hand sponson, the extra aerial base being visible externally.

Another type of set was employed when infantry tank co-operation reached a more sophisticated level than just hand signals or the use of various improvised methods with field telephones. This was the AN/VRC 3, an adaptation of the SCR 300 'Walkie Talkie'. The set was normally mounted on the left turret wall just in front of the loader's station, where it could be operated by the loader or the commander. The set had the same frequency band as the SCR 300 (40–48 mc) so that the tank crews could talk directly to the infantry. An additional method of communicating with the tank crew from outside the tank when it was 'buttoned-up' was via the RC 298 interphone extension kit. This comprised a handset, mounted in a small box, welded to the right rear of the hull.[19] Other methods of communications available were a set of flags (red, orange and green); flares (white, green and amber parachute flares); commander's spotlight and the vehicle siren.

OTHER MODELS

As the table on page 40 shows, there were

numerous other models of the Sherman, so it is relevant to look briefly at the history of the most important ones.

M4A2

It was late in 1941 that work started on a modified version of the M4, equipped with the General Motors 6046 diesel engine. This was the same engine as fitted to the M3A3 and comprised two GM truck engines mounted one each side of the engine compartment, each geared to a common propeller shaft. The tank was designated in December 1941, a pilot model produced in April 1942 and full production began the same month at both the Fisher Tank Arsenal and Pullman Standard Car Company. It was thus the first welded hull Sherman to enter production. Some of the early production M4A2s were still fitted with

View of fighting compartment with turret removed (Tank Museum).

The M4A2 model, which was similar to the M4 apart from never having a cast/rolled hull. This is a later production model with the modified vertical volute spring suspension, 47° front plate and larger driver's hatches. Note also added appliqué armour.

the two fixed .30-calibre MGs in the bow. They also had the early suspension system with the track return roller on top of each bogie. Later production models were fitted with an additional turret hatch for the loader and had their front hull sloped at 47° instead of the original 56°. The M4A2 was also built by the American Locomotive Company, Baldwin Locomotive Works and the Federal Machine and Welder Company, the total run of those equipped with the 75 mm gun numbering 8,053 from all five manufacturers. The M4A2 was used for training in USA and supplied to both the Soviet Union and Great Britain. With a few exceptions, the M4A2 was not used operationally by American forces, due to War Department policy that US troops would only be issued with petrol-engined tanks. As the table on page 40 shows, a further 2,915 M4A2s were produced, fitted with the 76 mm gun.

M4A3

Designated in January 1942, the first M4A3 tank was completed at the Ford Motor Company in late May 1942. This model was fitted with a Ford V8 petrol engine which had been

he M4A3 model with a
elded hull and one-
ece cast nose. Fitted
th the Ford GAA
trol engine, it was the
ost favoured type for
S Army use.

first tested in late 1941. Called the Ford GAA, it was the most promising tank engine developed at that time and the M4A3 became the preferred model for US Army service during the war and for a number of years after the war ended. It had a welded hull and a one-piece cast nose. Ford completed the run of 1,690 in September 1943; however, the major part of the M4A3 production came later with the M4A3 (75)W, M4A3(76)W, and M4A3(105),

which appeared from 1944 onwards and were built by various manufacturers. Their production amounted to a further 10,652 tanks, plus 254 of the heavily-armoured M4A3E2 'Jumbo' Sherman

M4A4

In order to meet production schedules, the Ordnance Committee approved the use of the Chrysler A 57 Multibank engine in February

The M4A4 had to be lengthened to take the Chrysler Multibank engine. The photo shows one of the pilot models at APG in May 1942.

1942 for the Sherman, and designated the welded-hull model, which was powered by this engine, as the M4A4. The complete run of 7,499 were built by the Detroit Tank Arsenal, ending in September 1943. The engine did have its problems, resulting from its complexity, as it was basically five Chrysler truck engines bolted together, thus having 30 cylinders and initially five belt-driven water pumps. Its size took up the majority of space in the enlarged engine compartment and made even simple maintainance difficult. Various changes (such as replacing the five water pumps with just one gear-driven pump) helped to get over some of these problems, as did an intensive training programme for maintenance personnel. In order to fit the larger engine the hull had to be lengthened by some 11 inches and the vertical fuel tanks removed. The loss of these tanks was compensated for by the installation of larger sponson tanks, each holding 80 gallons. Bulges also appeared – in the floor for the engine cooling fan and on the rear deck to house the upper part of the radiator assembly. To redistribute the weight properly the centre and rear bogies had to be relocated on the longer hull. Longer tracks were needed (83 plates per track instead of 79), and the ground contact length increased from 147 to 160 inches. The majority of M4A4s were allocated to the British, and a few were issued for training in the USA.

M4A6

Yet another new engine was developed, this time by the Caterpillar Tractor Company who modified the Wright G200 air-cooled radial engine to operate as a fuel-injected diesel. The engine was tried out in some M4A4 hulls in November 1942, which were designated as the M4E1. The tanks were shipped by Chrysler to Caterpillar for the installation of the new engine (designated by Ordnance as the RD-1820). Once all the 'bugs' had been sorted, production began at Chrysler, the first tank appearing in October 1943. However, only 75 were built and the production run was discontinued in February 1944, when it was decided to concentrate on petrol-engined models like the M4A3. The M4A6 used the later produc-

tion M4A4 hull, with a cast front section. It also had larger driver's and co-driver's hatches, a travelling lock for the 75 mm gun and appliqué armour welded over the sponson ammunition racks on each side of the hull.

Final basic model was the M4A6, pictured here on test at Fort Knox in March 1944. Only 75 were built.

60

FIRST COMBAT

As with the M3 it was the British Army who first used the M4 in action. Following the Gazala battles, Rommel had continued his advance and on 21 June 1942 his forces captured Tobruk. After pausing only to regroup, the DAK continued their advance driving the British back across the Egyptian frontier. At the time of the surrender of Tobruk, Winston Churchill was in Washington visiting President Roosevelt, so it was only natural that Roosevelt should offer to try to help his embattled ally. The first proposal was for 2nd Armored Division to be sent to assist. In his book *Hell on Wheels,* Donald E. Houston recalls that on 20 June 1942, the Armored Force ordered that all units should be ready to expect orders to move overseas at any time and that they must '. . . be prepared to execute these orders expeditiously and efficiently'. However, when General Marshal, Chief of Staff of the

US Army, looked at the situation more closely, it was clear that the division would take four to five months to reach Egypt, by which time it would be far too late to be of any use in stopping Rommel from reaching the Nile Delta. He therefore offered to withdraw 300 Shermans that had already been issued to units under training and send them immediately to Egypt.

This generous offer was accepted with alacrity and the convoy carrying the Shermans, together with 100 new M7 self-propelled howitzers, left the USA on 15 July. En route one of the ships was sunk by enemy submarines, but a special fast replacement was immediately despatched with a further 52 Shermans. By 11 September a total of 318 Shermans had arrived in Egypt. Although they were not in time to take part in the battle of Alam Halfa (31 August – 1 September) in which the British managed to halt the German advance on the El Alamein

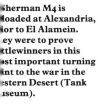

Sherman M4 is unloaded at Alexandria, prior to El Alamein. They were to prove battlewinners in this most important turning point to the war in the Western Desert (Tank Museum).

line, they were ready for the preparations that followed for the British counterstroke which was to prove the turning point in the desert war.

The Shermans were mainly M4A1s, but included some M4A2s, and as soon as they were unloaded work began to modify them for desert warfare, sandshields, for example, being added, before they were issued to units. The tank strength of the British Eighth Army just before the battle was 1,351, including 285 Shermans, 246 Grants and 167 Stuarts; of these 1,136 were with units in forward areas and 1,012 were fit for action. General Montgomery's outline plan was for the main thrust to be made by XXX Corps in the north with the task of forcing two corridors through the enemy minefields, then X Corps would pass through. In the south XIII Corps would mount two diversionary operations.

The first casualties to Sherman tanks were in 9th Armoured Brigade, who were supporting the infantry during the initial assault, and they were knocked out by mines and enemy anti-tank gunfire. This was also the case when the leading tanks of X Corps tried to deploy out of the cleared lanes through the enemy minefields. The first encounter by a Sherman with an enemy tank occurred the following morning, the 24th, shortly after sunrise, when leading elements of 2nd Armoured Brigade tangled with PzKpfw IIIs and IVs of the 15th Panzer Division. It was a long-range action, commencing at some 2,000 yards, and both sides suffered casualties before enemy tanks withdrew to the north.

FIRST AMERICAN ACTION

The first American troops to see action in Shermans were the crews of a single tank platoon of 6th Armored Regiment, 2nd Armored Division, which was attached to the 2nd Battalion, 13th Armored Regiment, 1st Armored Division, during the fighting south-west of Tébourba on 6 December 1942. 1st Armored Division, who were at that time equipped with M3s (see earlier account of their first action), bore the brunt of the fighting in Tunisia, while the 2nd Armored Division, who had landed at Casablanca, had the more modern M4 but saw little action. On 6 December, 1st Armored Division was operating south-west of Tébourba and had fallen back in the face of strong enemy attacks that morning. The Germans were now well forward and it was decided to mount a counter-attack to regain the lost terrain. Relatively fresh armoured forces were available, all of which, apart from a

knocking out most of the M3s and all the Shermans. As Colonel Henry E. Gardiner of Bozeman, Montana (who was later to command the 2nd Battalion after the then-CO was sent packing after this and other debacles), wryly put it in his diary: 'The first time they (meaning the 2nd Armored Division Shermans) went into action, they had all four tanks knocked out, so they cannot run over 88s either'. Colonel Gardiner had three tanks 'shot from under him' during those early battles in Tunisia; the first was an M3, but the other two were M4s. His comments are illuminating:

'... The second tank was an M4 which I lost to a German tank, its armor-piercing projectile penetrating the hull, killing the driver and wounding the assistant driver. The tank immediately burst into flames but the other two members of the crew and I escaped injury. My third tank to be destroyed was also an M4, which was hit in front by an anti-tank gun low down on the hull, killing three members of the crew. I was wounded, the fifth member of the crew escaping unscratched. The tank burned. One lesson we learned during our initial combat in and around Tébourba was to advance by leapfrogging. That meant that a platoon or a company would move out a short distance ahead of the company or battalion, while those units behind opened fire on every object that might conceal an anti-tank gun or tank. When the unit or units behind came up to those that had advanced initially, the process would be repeated.

'As soon as we returned to the Sbeitla area after the German withdrawal I inspected the remnants of the tanks that I had lost there and went to look over the battlefield at Sidi-bou-Zid. That is where the 2nd Battalion of the 1st Armored Regiment was completely destroyed in its first engagement. One could reconstruct exactly what happened. The concealed positions taken up by the German tanks and the anti-tank guns in a long row of big cactus plants and trees were still clearly visible. They had apparently held their fire until the 2nd Battalion, which was advancing in a roughly battalion front, were so close that every shot was a kill. The burned-out hulls of our tanks outlined the line of their advance...'

Sherman platoon (from 2nd Armored Division), had seen some action. However, their experience was very limited and they could really only be classified as green troops, especially as they were up against battle-hardened veterans of Rommel's Afrika Korps. The hurried way in which they went into the counter-attack, without any proper preparation and little knowledge of the locations of own and enemy troops, was indicative of their greenness. The well-positioned and camouflaged German tanks and anti-tank guns inflicted a devastating defeat on the American force,

Clearly it would be wrong to judge the effectiveness of the Sherman tank and of American armour, on this disastrous first en-

counter with the Germans. 1st Armored tankers had learnt their lessons the hard way and
went on to prove themselves and the battleworthiness of their Shermans in many subsequent engagements with the enemy.

Once full production got under way, the new
medium tank began to reach units in large
numbers and the Sherman rapidly became the
most widely used tank in the Allied Armies.
Over 17,000 were supplied to the British Army
alone, while the Russians received over 4,000.
The total number distributed under lend-lease
was 21,959 up to 1 September 1945. Undoubtedly the Sherman has to be one of the major
reasons why armour could justly claim the
lions' share of the credit for the eventual Allied
victory, with the tanks pre-eminent as the main
weapon of the land army.

The Sherman was used in battle all over the
world and to illustrate this use I have chosen a
selection of combat stories from the wealth of
material sent to me by ex-Sherman crewmen.
Although space does not permit more than just
a few reminiscences, the vividness with which
they convey graphically the operational use of
the Sherman tank and its crew, amply serves to
illuminate many of the subjects treated earlier
and later in this book in analytical and technical terms: They show the Sherman in its
element – a machine of war, operated by
human beings – a weapon system.

ITALY

William G. Haemmel served for three years

as loader in an M4 Sherman of the 3rd Platoon,
H Company, 1st Armored Regiment, 1st
Armored Division, US Army. He kept a diary
throughout his time in uniform, keeping it
with him on the tank and adding to it every
day. After the war he wrote a fascinating
account of his service life. To date it has never
been published although Bill Haemmel did
have a number of copies photocopied and he
very kindly sent me one. The following are
extracts from his book, the first being his
account of landing at Anzio. H Company had
been loaded at Naples on 24 January 1944, on
board a Royal Naval tank landing ship (LST
No 164), arriving off Anzio on the 26th. His
diary for the ensuing days reads as follows:

January 27, 1944, D-Day + 5
'We Land at Anzio
'The position of the Royal Navy's LST *164*
remained unchanged until 3 p.m. The harbor
was crowded with ships and more arrived. The
ducks – waterborne trucks – scurried from the
Liberty ships to shore. The port of Anzio
appeared to be undamaged and ships were
discharging across the docks. Men and
material streamed through the town.

'LST *164* was pulling into the Anzio docks
to disgorge its cargo when the Luftwaffe came
the closest to scoring upon the ship. The shore
was just a few hundred feet away when a ME
109 passed over the bow and travelled the
length of the ship. The pilot dropped his stack
of bombs 200 feet from the ship's side and was
gone with a roll of his wings. I caught a glimpse

of the pilot's head as he passed over the ship.

'Several of us were on deck when the final attack took place. While the ME 109 moved so fast we could no more than start for cover, the usual rain of flak which followed an attack propelled us on our way. I was the next to the last man to enter the narrow entrance to a flight of stairs leading below. A piece of flak hit the metal deck about five feet away from the entrance to the stairs. Metarazzo was right behind me and nearer to the flak. He was a small man but he actually picked me up and carried me through the entrance way and partway down the flight of stairs. Fortunately neither of us was hurt.

'We left LST 164 gladly. While the warmth and cleanliness of the ship were fine, we did not welcome being a target and only being able to jump and hide. While on ship we had eaten K rations which we prepared ourselves in the ship's galley. We could have joined the British crew but 1st Sgt Garren had an argument with the British mess man and he left us to our own devices. I was invited to one meal with the crew and I found their fare far below our standards. Although leaving the ship meant venturing

into greater peril, we happily ended our 34 hours on shipboard off the port of Anzio.

'The ship nosed up to the pier, opened wide its bow and we rolled out in a matter of minutes. The column of tanks went through the city and due north and then eastward into a large pine forest. Mosman reported the distance covered as six miles. Once we arrived we quickly removed the waterproofing hood and tape. The hood was secured to its base by clamps which opened with little effort. As the base had been welded to the exhaust outlet it would have to be removed at a later date. We covered the tank with our camouflage netting and threw our bed rolls on the ground.

'Each tank crew prepared its own C ration supper. We heated our cans over our Coleman stove and ate just as it was getting dark. At 6 p.m. we rolled up in our bed rolls and ended the day. We had strict orders against displaying any lights and there was nothing to do except go to sleep.

January 28 and 29, 1944

'For two days we sat and waited in the pine forest. There was little to do except complete the removal of the waterproofing and cart it away. It could not be said that we waited and watched – for we were in a world which appeared set apart from reality. We received no information or word about the situation but just sat and wondered about events. Allen and I were on company guard from 4 to 6.30 a.m. the first morning and the dark, silent woods made one feel alone and cut off in a hostile world. Daylight did not dispel the feeling. There was no distant sounds of battle – just an uneasy quiet hanging over everything.

'The air raids on the port at Anzio continued and several times we caught bare glimpses through the pine trees of Luftwaffe and RAF dog fights. Except for the battles being fought above us, there were no signs of combat around us. I walked to the edge of the forest the first afternoon and when I could see nothing returned the second afternoon for a longer walk. The open, rolling farm land northeast of the pine forest was quiet and peaceful in appearance. "Stand to" was the first sign of going into the attack, McNew explained as we got up

at 6.30 a.m., rolled up our bed rolls, checked our weapons and turned over the tank engine the second morning. When I returned from my hike that afternoon, McNew was relieved. The company had been placed on a 30 minute alert during my absence.

'At dusk we removed and loaded the camouflage net onto the back of the tank. The tanks lined up in a column. Late in the afternoon I Company went into combat and we listened on the battalion radio network as the attack made contact with the Germans. McNew explained that I was securing a line of departure for the battalion attack and he interpreted some of the information we received over the radio. I had encountered considerable resistance in infantry and Mark IV tanks. The advance ended with the daylight.

Sunday, January 30, 1944
The First Day of Battle

'At 3 a.m. McNew shook us into wakefulness. We secured our bed rolls to the rear platform of the tank and watched as Mosman

Bombing up. A Sherman crew loading ammunition into their Sherman. A total load ammo comprised 97 rounds of 75 mm, 300 rounds of .50 (if fitted) 4,750 rounds of .30, plu ammo for personal weapons, grenades, et

66

followed McNew's motioned commands to draw the tank close to the rear of the tank immediately in front. Once the company had assembled in a march column, the pause was short. The first tank moved out and the others followed in as tight a formation as possible.

'The night was moonless and clear. Once the pine forest fell behind and vision improved, the distance between tanks was increased. Both Mosman and McNew settled further into the protection of the tank. The springs on the drivers seat sang out as Mosman adjusted the elevation of his seat and shifted his bulk.

'The tank column moved westward out of the forest and then northward up the Albano Road, sometimes called the Via Anziate. A turn to the west and the company halted and dispersed in a field. I was detailed to stand turret guard and remained standing while the others settled themselves as best they could inside the tank. A thin grey line proclaimed the start of the day.

'Suddenly, with a whooshing, whining sound, ending in a sharp flat roar, several German shells struck a hundred yards up the road. The flash of the exploding shells appeared bright and close; involuntarily, I ducked my head into the turret. There was no additional "incoming mail" at the moment.

'The pause in the field lasted almost an hour. Then the tanks pulled back onto the road and re-formed the column as the day dawned. The road ascended a slight hill and beyond, the Alban hills loomed dark and ominous. The sense of loneliness fell away as the day advanced. Silently, cautiously a column of infantry passed up the road. They labored under their weapons and ammunition, carrying mortars, machine guns, bazookas and all their accouterments. The 3rd Battalion, 6th Armored Infantry moved up and over the crest of the hill. To the northward, toward the German positions, the view became obscured as a smoke curtain descended over the sea.

'Suddenly the first tank in the line moved forward. McNew slapped me lightly to draw my attention and directed me to assume my post and to "hook up" with the tank intercommunication system. "Duck Buggy" rolled forward over the crest of the hill at 7.15 a.m. The company of tanks moved from the road column and formed a front or line; the 1st Platoon on the right, the 2nd in the center and the 3rd on the left. The approach march was finished and the company had formed on

the line of departure and was in the proper jumping off position. As the 3rd moved across to the left flank of the company front, the 1st and 2nd began to fire and the staccato roar of the tank cannons punctuated the air.

'The company line was along the top of a ridge and immediately upon the skyline. The ground gradually dropped away for several miles and then gradually ascended into the foothills of the Alban Hills. The area was creased with gullies which generally ran southwest-northeast. The main river in the area was the Moletta which flowed generally from east to west. Occasionally a tributary ran at right angles to the main river. The direction of the attack was to the northeast, astride the ridges between the various gullies. There was little if any vegetation. Stone houses were scattered about the area and offered the only cover. About 300 yards in front of our tank three houses were clustered together. Following a brief consultation with McNew, Croom fired several rounds of high explosive into the houses. The firing died down and all became quiet. There was no return fire – only an uneasy silence. The order to advance was delayed.

'The quiet inside the tank was profound. McNew slowly, carefully and methodically surveyed the terrain with his field glasses, sweeping from side to side. He was careful to expose as little of himself as possible; only his steel helmet placed on top of his tank helmet and the field glasses showed above the rim of the turret hatch. Croom sat hunched over his gunner's controls and chain smoked. His gaze was fixed to the gun periscope and he sometimes moved the turret. Mosman's eyes were closed and he prayed, telling his beads, I alternated between scanning the scene with my periscope and borrowing McNew's field glasses for a sweep of the horizon. I noted that Croom's hands trembled as he lighted one cigarette from another.

'"Don't you get used to all this, Leon?" I inquired. "With your combat experience, I'd suppose you would be by now." The Arkansan snorted: "Hell, no. You can't get used to bein' scared. It gets worse and worse all the time. There are just some things you can never get used to, and bein' scared is one."

'McNew had directed that I throw the empty shell cases out of the turret port hole. As a result, when I expressed my need to relieve myself, there were no shells to use as a receptacle. McNew and I carefully climbed out of the turret. We had turned to re-enter when a sniper opened fire upon us. The bullet whined close by. I dived head first over the rim of the turret hatch and McNew scrambled in on my heels. Croom sent 12 rounds slamming into the houses.

'The quiet returned. The anxiety increased and the waiting seemed interminable. The needs of hunger were satisfied by a few K ration biscuits and some water from a canteen. Several of the crew simply did not eat.

'The terrain before the line of silent tanks gradually disappeared from view as a smoke screen settled down. The pall moved to the southwest and slowly enveloped the tanks. "Can't see a Goddamn thing," commented Croom to no one in particular.

'The slowly drifting smoke obscured all sides and the companion tanks were lost to view. McNew strained to detect any sound of movement but everything continued quiet. The radio reported no movement. Slowly, quietly, with the same spectral effect with which it had come, the smoke cleared away.

'Promptly at 10 a.m. the line of tanks started forward and the attack was under way! McNew instructed Croom to fire on the houses and once a few shells had crashed into the buildings, Mosman was ordered to move forward. As McNew's tank advanced our section's other tank, commanded by Stump, laid down cannon fire to cover our movement. Once McNew's tank had reached a protected position and the tank was "hull down," or hidden in part by the contour of the terrain, Croom would open fire and Stump's tank would move up. Alternately pausing to fire and advancing without firing, the tank line moved forward. The two tank sections leap-frogged the drive forward. SSgt. Hinzman and Sgt. Cochran repeated the action to the left of the 1st Section. The platoon lieutenant's tank sometimes worked with the 1st Section and sometimes with the 2nd. The roar of the motors was punctuated by the "slam" of the tank cannons and the roar of the machine guns.

'The Germans were completely unseen; it was as if they were not present. The tank attack moved forward.

'The company radio net carried the orders of Hillenmeyer in the company command tank. He directed the advance of the company line and coordinated the attack of all three platoons. Late in the morning, while crossing a gully, the turret hatch cover snapped shut, breaking two bones in Hillenmeyer's right hand. Lt. Abrams of the 1st Platoon assumed command of the company.

'At noon the company advance slowed. The attack had gained a mile against light infantry opposition. McNew's tank had "shot-up" a number of houses and advanced from one "hull-down" position to another. I kept the tank cannon loaded and supplied the machine gun and had been able to maintain a constant survey with my periscope. For a few fleeting moments a German machine gun crew had appeared. I loaded the cannon and looked again and the German machine gun crew was gone. Otherwise the enemy was not in evidence to me.

'A few biscuits and water served to satisfy the few crew members who were hungry, including myself.

'In the afternoon the advance was resumed. McNew carefully picked out the positions where his tank paused and with equal care he directed a steady volume of fire at all possible points where the Germans might find cover.

'The tank moved over the crest of the hill next to an irrigation ditch, nosed downward and stuck fast! The front of the tank was pointed down and the rear up, exposing the top of the tank to the Germans. Mosman frantically tried to move the tank forward, backward or slip sideways, all to no avail. McNew dismounted and reported the tank front was

A Kangaroo APC, converted from a late model Ram tank carrying Canadian infantry in north-west Europe. It could hold section of 11 men in battle order, plus a cr of two.

caught fast in the mire. The crew could not extricate the vehicle. The company line of tanks moved past and disappeared. The sound of gunfire rolled back. Otherwise the battle appeared miles away.

'An hour later the tank of Sgt. Mees pulled "Duck Buggy" free. Two cables were extended between the tanks and the pull was sufficient to dislodge McNew's tank. Both tanks returned to the company and resumed the attack.

' "Croom, put a round into the open window on the second storey," McNew directed, indicating a house to the left front. "I think I saw some movement there. Mosman, move to the right some, I don't want to have our side face that house." Smoke boiled out the open windows and door as several shells found their mark and the tank moved past. Nothing else moved.

'As the afternoon drew to a close the advance slowed and finally halted. The advance had covered about two and one-half miles. I reported that only four rounds of high explosive ammunition remained. McNew directed that a raking machine gun fire be maintained to our front and four boxes of 30 caliber ammo were discharged. The gun overheated and the firing stopped. The company of tanks made a ragged line; several tanks were advanced more than others and two or three tanks projected from the irregular line. The company retired several hundred yards, pulling back and to the right. Wherever possible, the individual tanks simply backed up so that the more heavily armored front faced to the Germans. If the tank had to turn about, the turret was reversed in order that the turret front was maintained toward the enemy. The 3rd Battalion, 6th Armored Infantry Regiment was digging in and the tank company served as an outpost line to cover the infantry as they entrenched. McNew's tank and several others maintained a cover of machine gun fire. Several M-5 light tanks from A moved up and joined the firing. The infantrymen moved swiftly, taking advantage of whatever cover the terrain offered. Foxholes and weapons emplacements quickly appeared. The infantrymen either lay upon their sides or crouched low and swung their small hand picks and shovels. The dirt flew and a network of holes appeared.

'Dusk was rapidly settling in when the tanks carefully withdrew. As vision became more and more limited, the tank commanders personally guided their vehicles through the infantry positions. Once the tanks were clear, the column was re-formed and the company returned to a point on the road perhaps one mile to the rear of the initial stopping place in the early morning. The exhausted crew members dropped down for some rest and sleep. Several unstrapped their blankets or bedrolls and stretched out next to or under the tanks, trying to sleep and fight off the cold. Others tried to find relaxed positions in the tanks.

'Shortly after the men had made themselves comfortable the trucks from the regimental Service Company arrived. The individual five gallon cans of 90 octane gasoline had been filled from large tank trucks miles from the front line and stacked into "6 × 6" two and one-half ton trucks. Other trucks had loaded crated rounds of 75 mm shells and boxes of 30 caliber machine gun ammunition. The truck driver and assistant driver unloaded the cargo as rapidly as they could and then roared down the road away from the front lines.

'All five members of the tank crew formed an irregular "bucket brigade" and handed the gas from the ground to the tank and into the tank. While Mosman fed the gasoline into the tank, I received the ammunition and strapped each round into its place or piled it on the floor of the turret. While the five of us were gray and haggard with fatigue and would occasionally snap and snarl at each other in the course of the work, in less than an hour the job was done. The camouflage net was unrolled and pulled over the tank. I noted it was 9 p.m. as I dropped back into my bed roll. In an instant I was fast asleep.'

TUNISIA

The second extract from Haemmel's book concerns a typical duel between a Sherman troop, led by Lieut Jim E. Tracy, and an enemy anti-tank gun. It shows very clearly that the soldiers of 1st Armored Division had learned their basic lessons well in Tunisia.

'During the early part of the Tuscan advance Capt. Hillenmeyer served as Regimental Motor Officer. At the time Tracy's platoon was serving as the point for Task Force C, Hillenmeyer was following the point platoon about a thousand yards to the rear. He had his jeep's radio tuned in on Tracy's net. As the five tanks moved up to the crest of a hill, Hillenmeyer heard Tracy speak on the radio: "Hold up, all stations. I don't like the looks of this." Tracy suspected the Germans might have a trick ready for the advancing Americans. Hillenmeyer described the events as follows: "All tanks stopped before showing themselves on the skyline. I saw Tracy dismount. He crawled up to the crest of the hill, and spent a long time flat on his belly deliberately scanning the terrain ahead with his field glasses. As soon as he found what he was looking for, he motioned to his tank commanders. They all dismounted and one by one crawled to the top of the hill to see what Tracy pointed out to them. Then back to the tanks they ran, jumped in, and ducked down in the turrets. I had done the same thing often enough to know what was taking place. Tracy had spotted some kind of target, and the tank commanders were now giving instructions to their gunners so that they would be ready to fire as soon as they poked their muzzles over the crest.

'In a few minutes each tank commander had his right arm straight up in the air – our traditional signal which meant, "I am ready to move out." Tracy's clipped command came over the radio: "Move out." It was perfectly executed. Five tanks hit the crest of that hill simultaneously, and five 75s blasted away within ten seconds of each other. Tracy was never one to waste words. There was no emotion in his voice as he said flatly, "That's all for him. Move out." A few minutes later I followed the road over the crest of that hill and down into a valley where a bridge crossed over a little stream. Sticking straight up in the air out of a clump of bushes beside that bridge was an antitank gun which looked like a telephone pole – sure death for five tanks except for the fact that these tanks had been led by Lt. Jim E. Tracy. He knew the Germans' habits, and his instinct had told him that somewhere down there a gun would be waiting for him. As I rolled across the bridge, I saw the bodies of several Germans strewn about. They never got to fire a shot.'

ank recovery vehicle
31 raising a Sherman
t of a ditch near
euwstad, Holland,
ctober 1944.

THE PACIFIC THEATRE

Switching to the other side of the world, here is a short extract from the history of the 44th Tank Battalion, which fought in the South Pacific. It deals with the operations of A Company on Leyte:

'Company "A" was the only organization of the battalion continually employed through the operation in tank-infantry team roles. The first five days of the landing were spent in the vicinity of San Fernando attached to the 12th Cavalry Regiment, 1st Cavalry Division. On 26 October the company moved to Palo from where reconnaissance by tank patrols took place to the West and South of Palo. Next stop for the men and tanks was Alangalang followed by a move to the vicinity of Carigara on 6 November. From here on out "A" Company had not only to battle the enemy but fight conditions which hampered every move. The mud and tank terrain were probably the most difficult that the 44th men encountered. Three steps in any direction put one knee deep in mud. From November 6, when the first tanks made their now famous "Amphibious hop" 200 yards out into Carigara Bay in order to bypass a deep, swollen stream, until December 21st, there was almost continuous contact with the fanatical enemy. Concealed Japs in fox holes were always a menace and one succeeded in throwing a satchel charge on the tank rear deck, ripping up the top engine compartment doors and damaging the engines severely. On this tank, doing third echelon work, the maintenance crew began work that had to be done under trying conditions and sometimes with the whizz of bullets flying close by. The battle of "Breakneck Ridge" on 11 November found "A" Company tanks and men in the thick of the fight. Starting the advance without infantry, intense enemy fire was encountered.

71

Everything was thrown at the Japs but most effective were hand grenades and 45 sub machine gun fire delivered by tank commanders from the turret. Twenty infantrymen advanced but were unable to hold the ground the tanks had won. Forced to withdraw, one tank backed off the narrow trail, got stuck and slipped over a steep embankment. The crew evacuated and the tank was destroyed to keep it from falling into enemy hands. Dismounting from his tank, Capt. J. P. Vanwinkle was assisting the platoon leader when he was wounded in the side and hand and evacuated. This same day the half track carrying the Liaison officer, Major Barkspale, was ambushed and sprayed with automatic fire but the Major was the only one hit, suffering a slight wound.

'Breakneck Ridge was taken later by the tanks of the 1st platoon and infantry and the tankers were credited with 250 Japs killed. One particular Jap met his Waterloo one morning as he moved up to Sgt John L. King's tank with a grenade in either hand. King, in the turret at the time was just throwing out a cigarette butt when he spotted the Nip. He dove for his sub machine gun and when he came up the Jap had laid one grenade down and was puffing on the cigarette. That was his last smoke.

'The tanks continued firing at all types of targets and in turn encountered mines, snipers, mortar, machine gun and 75 mm artillery fire. Some of the boys in the kitchen had a close call when Jap artillery started landing in the area. Lawrence and Stayton, seeking shelter behind a big stump, decided it was too close to the road and took off for a creek bed. Returning later they found the stump half shot away and punctured with holes. Two others, found refuge back of the stoves which warded off shell fragments while taking some dents and punctures.

'Some kitchen utensils and cans of bully beef and a 3/4 ton were also among the targets hit. On the 14th of November the Japs attacked another tank with satchel charges, blowing off a track and jamming the escape hatch. The crew was evacuated after all guns were disabled, radio crystals and important accessories removed. Despite assurance of the infantry that the tank would be outposted during the night, the next day found it completely destroyed. Soon after, engaging an enemy tank and artillery field piece, a bad lot of ammo was uncovered, 80% of the 75's being duds. In

A fully-tracked Prime Mover M33 towing an inch gun.

spite of it, the artillery was knocked out. Two of our tanks took direct hits without damage.

'The Japs in an amphibious landing caused quite a bit of anxiety when they cut the MSR of the troops fighting to Ormoc. They set up a road block consisting of our own 75 ammunition still in the clover leaf containers, with explosives attached. Our own tanks continued to run into faulty ammunition, 80% to 90% being duds, but managed to break the road block. After breaking through, the tanks and infantry continued on East of Pinamopoan and found a convoy of five vehicles including two ambulances, shot up and the occupants, including litter cases killed. A little farther on the infantry dug in and the tanks returned to their area. Hoping to get away from a bit of the mud, Sgt Scaglion, and Cpl Bennett with a few others returned by truck to the Battalion area at Tunga to pick up ammo and mail. On the return trip they fought a losing fight with the muddy roads and when the truck got stuck they returned to the Battalion in the rain. Col. Ross spotted two of the mud and rain soaked boys and invited them in his tent to get warmed up. When he turned around, there were all seven of them, but in spite of the surprisingly large number the colonel was good to his word and soon two quarts of his private stock were just empty bottles.

'On 27 November another Jap artillery piece and also a tank were destroyed. One platoon of tanks this same day was ordered into the northern edge of Limon. As they approached the enemy opened up with a heavy concentration of artillery fire. Lt. Leo F. Reinartz, acting company commander, left his shelter and ran towards the approaching tanks to warn them to turn back. Disregard of his own safety, led to his death as a shell fell just behind him. The fragments wounded him fatally in the back and he died without regaining consciousness. He was the first officer of the battalion to give his life for his country.

'Area fire and direct support of the infantry continued to occupy the tankers. On 18 December another enemy tank and two enemy field pieces were destroyed. The Japs continued shelling the tanks and area at various times. On 19 December the company was released but due to road conditions other tanks could not reach the area and "A" Company men continued the fighting, advancing against heavy Jap fire. One tank was set afire by two Molotov cocktails and the crew forced to evacuate, but the tank was recovered and withdrawn under its own power with only slight damage. Throughout the campaign, "A" Company not only took part in offensive action, but had to continually be on the alert for infiltration, especially at night. Twenty one Japs were killed trying to get to the tanks and tankers. In all, "A" Company killed over 1000 Japs besides destroying road blocks, enemy tanks, artillery, machine guns and emplacements.'

NORTH-WEST EUROPE

The remainder of the chapter comprises some extracts from the history of the 6th Armored Division, which served in North West Europe as part of General George Patton's great US Third Army. They are taken from *The Super Sixth* by George F. Hofmann, who has very kindly allowed me to quote them.

The first concerns operations by Combat Command B in the vicinity of Lanfroicourt, France, in the area of the Gremecy Forest in late September 1944. It was usual for an armoured division to comprise five 'commands' under divisional control – CCA, CCB, CCR, Artillery Command and Trains Command. The first three were the combat ele-

ments and comprised a balanced mix of armour and armoured infantry, plus supporting arms, tailored for the job in hand.

'At 0700 on 22 September CCB moved out in two columns through a heavy morning fog. The south column was to move through Alincourt, Manhoue and then on to Lanfroicourt.

'The north column was to move through Han and then to Armaucourt. Within a half hour the north column contacted the Germans at Armaucourt after crossing the Seille River at Han. Company C, 69th Tank Battalion, which was spearheading the north column, encountered enemy artillery, anti-tank weapons, and infantry equipped with panzerfausts just to the west of Armaucourt. The German defense was quickly dispatched but when the company passed to the east of the town, the Germans opened up with tank fire, and knocked out the lead tank, commanded by Captain Thompson,

the Company Commander. Behind Thompson's tank was Lieutenant Lawrence J. Parziale who immediately engaged the German tanks and knocked them out. About the same time, from approximately two hundred yards, Lieutenant Taylor's lead tank of the 2nd platoon was knocked out severely wounding a number of the crewmen. Lieutenant Carl Clark, Jr., seeing the wounded crewmen, pouring out of Taylor's smoking tank, stopped to give aid and his tank was knocked out. Lieutenant Robert J. Nathan, from the 3rd platoon, started around the disabled tanks when his tank was hit and put out of commission. While the rest of C Company tanks skirted over a nearby hill to avoid enemy fire, and locate the German tanks, Nathan and Clark aided and evacuated the wounded tankers.

'As soon as the three tanks became disabled, Sergeants Sherman C. Cahal and George

An M12 155 mm Gun Motor Carriage of U: Third Army in action near Echternach, Luxembourg, on 8 February 1945. Only : were built.

Marie moved their tanks toward the German fire and located three enemy tanks. Flanking the German position, Cahal and Marie knocked out three German tanks and eliminated a number of accompanying infantrymen.

'Three of C Company's officers were seriously wounded and communication was disrupted. The column was halted by four smoking tanks. Major Chester E. Kennedy and Lieutenant Parziale reorganized the column and led the remainder through heavy German fire toward its attack position facing Amance Hill from the north.

'The south column also met stiff resistance south of Manhoue where the Germans blew the bridge, causing the column to detour to the north route behind the reserve elements and cross at Han. Company D, 69th Tank Battalion, moved into Armaucourt and, after heavy fighting captured the town, including the CO of the German 381st Panzer Grenadier Battalion. The tankers then moved ahead and into Lanfroicourt and secured the town after light opposition.

'In the short period, D Company tankers along with one platoon from C Company, 603rd Tank Destroyer Battalion and one platoon from C Company, 25th Armored Engineer Battalion, captured hundreds of prisoners and destroyed numerous vehicles.

'Combat Command B, less two batteries of the 212th Armored Field Artillery Battalion which were left on the north side of the Seille River in support, closed at 1950 positioning themselves north of Amance Hill, the objective. Read's maneuver placed the German

defenders on the hill in an untenable situation; CCB was positioned to their north, the 35th Division faced them from the south and the 80th Division from the west.

'During the night considerable enemy movement south of CCB was detected. Apparently the Germans were trying to escape from the trap. Troop B, 86th Cavalry Reconnaissance Squadron, moving to intercept the retreating Germans, attempted unsuccessfully to block a main escape route. German infantry and tanks blunted B Troop's effort to block the main road and Corps artillery support was requested to interdict the area after tactical air support was denied. Combat Command B did manage to capture a small group of retreating Germans and freed one officer from the 134th Infantry Regiment, 35th Infantry, who had been captured the night before.

'Under the three-pronged pressure, the Germans abandoned Amance Hill and tried to disengage themselves. At 0715 on the 23rd CCB received word that its attack on Amance Hill was cancelled since the pressure caused by the movement down from the northeast enabled the 35th Infantry Division to attack the hill at dusk on the 22nd and capture it without difficulty. Read then received orders to move a Task Force to Leyr which was positioned near a major crossroad used by the retreating Germans. The 44th Armored Infantry Battalion (minus two Rifle Companies) with a Reconnaissance Company, 603rd Tank Destroyer Battalion, one medium tank company, one light tank platoon, and one tank destroyer platoon, moved out and attacked the town. Shortly after, it was taken and outposted. At the same time another Task Force from CCB consisting of tanks from B Company, 69th Tank Battalion, and attached cavalry, engineers, and tank destroyers, was ordered to move to the vicinity of Arraye-et-Han and block the highway west of the town. The Task Force was met by intensive enemy mortar and artillery fire.

'The tankers from C Company had moved out in line to a defiladed position on the high ground east of the road to Armaucourt. Lieutenant George E. Copeland moved his platoon into position to cover the road from Armaucourt to Arraye-et-Han while Lieutenant Donald Bedwell's platoon continued in line and moved to the right of Copeland's tanks. His mission was to establish a field of fire and cover the direct front. Later, after the platoons

rossing the bridge over e River Mulda at ochlicts, after PoWs een on left) had eared away a adblock, this late odel M4A1, with mm gun, belonging to h Armored Division, eeds on into ermany.

were in positions, James F. Morris, the CO, moved a section of Bedwell's tanks to the high ground north of the Arraye-et-Han highway so the tanks could deliver direct fire on the enemy-held town. Bedwell, who had the center tank, picked targets at large in the town and opened fire. Sergeant Palm, on Bedwell's right, aimed and fired into a boundary left of a church steeple located in the center of the town while Sergeant Sheppard, on Bedwell's left, picked the boundary to the right of the church steeple and opened up. The firing was executed without drawing German fire due to close reconnaissance and quick fire and movement. But the Germans were concerned with the fire from Bedwell's tanks, and when it became dark they launched a small infantry counterattack with machine guns. The attack was repulsed and the engineer platoon which was guarding Bedwell's flank captured a number of prisoners. Meanwhile, B Company, 44th Armored Infantry Battalion, reinforced the tankers but were hit hard by artillery fire as they moved into position. Early the next morning the Germans again counterattacked but this time with a larger force. Several friendly vehicles were knocked out by an anti-tank gun but again the attack stalled. A third attack was nipped at 1000. Bedwell knocked out a German tank and personnel from the B Company's Headquarters section aided on the kill by burning the tank and killing the escaping crew members.

'At 1430 the tankers and attached units were relieved by elements of the 35th Infantry Division. The tired and worn out tankers returned to an assemble area southwest of Lanfroicourt.

'Grow[20] did not interfere with Read's attack against the German pocket on the 22nd, but did keep track of the operation as the rest of the division moved into Gremecy Forest. Grow considered Read's crossing of the Seille River at Han against determined resistance a tactical feat, but Read stoically found nothing unusual in the operation. He considered it standard-operating-procedure to seize bridges and to seek fords to expedite CCB's operations. Read anticipated the Germans would destroy all existing bridges and consequently fords were the next best bet, such as existed at Han. As Read would say "This was one of those operations you played by ear. Since we were never sure in advance exactly what effect the terrain or enemy reaction might have on our oper-

ations, we always remained flexible and ready for any contingency." Read found it easy to shift his task forces if the situation required. Thus, in moving behind the Germans on Amance Hill, CCB was in a position to reinforce success as rapidly as possible, bypassing difficult terrain, and causing the enemy to be pinched out.'

The next extract from *The Super Sixth* concerns the crossing of the Nied River in November 1944.

'The 6th Armored Division, in four columns, continued its attack on a ten mile front toward the swollen Nied River on the 11th. When the columns moved out early that morning, there were indications that finally clear weather was at hand. The 6th Armored Division hit the Nied in four places, reading from the south, CCA at Baudrecourt (TF 68) and Han-sur-Nied (TF 9). These were both supported by the doughs of the 80th Infantry Division. Then to the north, Read's CCB hit the Nied Francais at Remilly (TF 50) and Sanry-sur-Nied (TF 15).

'At 0700 on the 11th, friendly artillery opened up on the town of Bechy, located less than a few miles west from the Nied River. Ten minutes later Godfrey moved out his Task Force and by 0900 had cleared the mines barring entry into the town and engaged dug-in enemy riflemen. The resistance was tough but TF 9 and the doughs from the 317th Infantry managed to continue their advance toward the Nied River under heavy German artillery fire. To make matters worse, a few planes from tactical air, identified as P-47's, strafed Godfrey's column between Bechy and Han-sur-Nied knocking out a jeep-displaying an identification panel.

'The advance guard, composed of a company of infantry, a platoon of tank destroyers, a platoon of M5's and a platoon of Sherman tanks, rumbled toward the high ground overlooking Han-sur-Nied from the west. When elements from B Company, 68th Tank Battalion, got close to the ridge overlooking Han, the tanks deployed in the woods adjacent to the road in line of platoons. The tankers soon determined that the bridge was still intact but prepared for demolition.

'Immediately word went back to Godfrey's CP regarding the intact bridge. At the CP located in the woods just short of the ridge overlooking the bridge were Hines, Godfrey,

Captain Ross C. Brown, CO of B Company, 68th Tank Battalion, and Lieutenant Daniel Nutter, CO, 1st Platoon, B Company, 25th Armored Engineer Battalion. Godfrey ordered Nutter, who had just returned from a mine-marking detail, to check the approach to the bridge for mines and explosives. Brown radioed Lieutenant Vernon L. Edwards, CO, 1st Platoon, B Company, to take his tanks across the intact bridge.

'While Nutter and his engineers were racing toward the bridge, Brown's tankers noticed several hundred German vehicles withdrawing east. German truck and horse-drawn artillery were desperately trying to cross the river. The tankers placed direct fire on the retreating Germans with their MG's and tank guns. It was apparent that the Germans were disorganized and not manning their gun positions, but T. F. Godfrey's advance guard needed more firepower, such as artillery, tank destroyers and medium tanks. In short order the Germans began to realize the severity of the situation

and started to organize their defenses. By 1400 the Germans had placed over a dozen 20 mm anti-aircraft guns in position along the road running west out of Han-sur-Nied.

'By now Edwards' platoon was in an assault position on the crest of the ridge overlooking the river. The platoon composed of four tanks (the fifth tank having been knocked out in earlier action) was split into two sections. The first section, composed of Sergeant Hubert W. Zaumbrecker's tank and Edwards' tank, would make the attempt to cross over the wooden bridge while the second section, composed of Staff Sergeant Everett H. Tourjee's tank and Sergeant Robert L. Hume's tank, would offer covering fire. At about 1430, Zaumbrecker's tank ran the gauntlet of German fire and crossed the bridge into Han. Then Edwards' went across firing its tank weapons. At the west side of the river, about half a dozen Germans armed with panzerfausts attempted to stop the tanks. Edwards raised up from the turret of his Sherman and fired his grease-gun at the Ger-

77

mans as his tank raced over the bridge. On the far side of the bridge, on the ramp, Edwards' tank stopped. Twenty millimeter anti-aircraft fire from the high ground to the northeast cut down Edwards and he died almost instantly; his body slumped down into the turret, jamming the 75 mm gun guard. Zaumbrecker, who crossed before Edwards, pulled up along side the first house in the town of Han, approximately thirty to fifty yards from the bridge.

'In the meantime, the second section started for the bridge, but just before reaching the approach, Hume's tank was hit and caught fire. Events moved fast. German fire became intense. Nutter, who was sent to check the approach to the bridge for mines and explosives, hit the crest of the hill with Sergeant Paul Lukart, T/5 Charles Cunningham, T/5 Ira Zimmerman, and T/4 Cleo Garringer. Moving in leaps and bounds along a drainage ditch next to the road, the engineers who were wearing flak jackets arrived at a crossroad and railroad forty to fifty yards from the bridge. The Germans were well dug-in, in foxholes on both sides of the river. From the railroad running along the west bank of the river, the German infantry fired at the backs of the engineers and infantry approaching the west span. Nutter yelled, "Come on," and he and Cunningham dashed to the road block in front of the bridge and noticed Edwards' stalled tank on the far ramp. Also Hume's smoking tank was parked at the approach to the bridge and Tourjee's tank was farther back and off to the side. Nutter dashed across the bridge and kicked about three demolition charges, scattering them. He dashed back towards the friendly side at the same time infantrymen charged across towards the enemy side. Immediately the Germans opened up with small arms fire and a few infantrymen dropped. When Nutter reached the friendly side, small arms fire was hitting on the bridge from both sides of the river. Nutter turned to Cunningham, "Leave the mine detector and help me cut these charges." Borrowing a trench knife and a pocket knife from an infantryman, the two started across the bridge cutting charges. Nutter reached the far side but Cunningham was pinned down about half way across. The wires were cut and the bridge was saved and Nutter and Cunningham raced back to the friendly side. Again infantrymen attempted to cross and were cut down. Nutter, now operating

against the odds, crossed again with additional infantrymen and took shelter behind the medium tank that was still sitting on the far ramp. All were killed or wounded except Nutter, who helped one man who was hit get behind the tank. Again the Lieutenant dashed across to the friendly side, but time ran out. He was hit in the head and fell at the end of the bridge on the ramp, blocking the tank approach to the bridge. Cunningham rushed over to the fallen Lieutenant and pulled him by the hands about ten yards to the road block, but it was too late; the head wound was fatal.

'From the time Zaumbrecker's and Edwards' tanks raced across the span and Nutter and Cunningham cut the demolition wires, events moved very fast. Tourjee managed to move his Sherman across the bridge with three infantrymen hanging on the back of the tank under the deck and flat against the engine compartment door. When he reached the other side he was told he was in command of the platoon, now consisting of three tanks. The tanks deployed in Han with the infantrymen, but it would be at least three hours before more would get across.

'The Germans, who were unable to destroy the bridge, increased their fire to a furious pace in order to blunt the small bridgehead. German artillery, flak, rocket launchers, and small arms were directed to the wooden span. Officers and enlisted men from TF 9 and the 317th Infantry began to fall in numbers, causing the attack to stall. Lieutenant Colonel Sterling Burnette, CO of the 317th, received a mortal wound. Hines, the CO of CCA, seeing the attack blunted from the hill overlooking the river, raced down the slope toward the embattled bridge to encourage the doughs who were leaderless because of casualties suffered by their officers. Before he went down to the bridge, Hines, in his observation post next to the road overlooking the river, drew German 20 mm tracer fire every time he observed the action below. "I could see the individual rounds coming right at me; every time I had a fraction of a second to spare to dive into my foxhole," Hines explained. "Then when we laid smoke in front of the Germans directing the fire, I had no trouble in finding out whether or not the covering fire was effective. I simply stood straight up and because for the first time the Germans did not shoot at me, I knew right away they could not see over here any longer."

'Hines rushed into Godfrey's CP, which

arrived on the hill overlooking the Nied, and ordered Godfrey to lead the troops across the bridge. Very calmly Godfrey looked at the charged-up CCA commander and retorted that he had to stay at the CP and direct operations. Hines retorted, "Then I'll do it," and jumped into his jeep and raced down the hill.

'Hines was able, under heavy enemy fire, to lead and direct across the bridge and into Han-sur-Nied one hundred riflemen to reinforce the small contingent of troops and tanks that already had negotiated the one hundred foot treacherous span.

'Meanwhile, the 231st Armored Field Artillery Battalion had moved up to support the crossing. The Reconnaissance Section of B Battery, which rode the point, caught an 88 mm round which entered the right front side and killed Pfc. Leonard O. Taggart, considered by B Battery as the best dressed soldier to ever enter the unit and the classiest guidon bearer in the army. The rest of the reconnaissance section sustained minor injuries. Lieutenant Colonel Thomas M. Crawford's artillerymen from Missouri delivered continuous concentrations of high explosives and white phosphorous on the German positions, making it possible for the small number of troops who had crossed the river to hold. Hines later recalled that the 231st "gave

us great support."

'Though the artillerymen of the 231st provided covering fire, it did not discourage the Germans from reacting. Enemy artillery continued. A 150 mm round struck near the bridge where Hines was directing the crossing and a piece of shrapnel entered his cheek.

'At 1620 an organized assault to reinforce the bridgehead was begun. This was proceeded by a 15-minute artillery preparation which included smoke. By dark some one hundred infantrymen had crossed over the bridge. Shortly thereafter light and medium tanks began to rumble across. After darkness the remaining troops of T. F. Godfrey, as well as a regiment of the 80th Infantry Division, had occupied Han-sur-Nied. During the night the town was mopped up and an attack by the doughs of the 317th Infantry cleared the ridge beyond the town.'

The third quotation from *The Super Sixth* is taken from the period later in November 1944, when 6th Armored was advancing towards yet another river barrier – the Mutterbach River.

'While advancing east along route N 74, B Company, 15th Tank Battalion, encountered a force of German tanks on the south edge of Diffembach-les-Hellimer. Some of the tanks were positioned between houses and were waiting for Lagrew's tankers. Very shortly a tank vs tank engagement ensued resulting in three destroyed German tanks which were surrounded and systematically eliminated; but it cost B Company three of their own tanks. The Germans then withdrew the remainder of their armor along the main road to the high ground east of town and began to fire into the 2nd Battalion, 137th Infantry, who were attempting to mop up the village.

'The largest column of Lagrew's force advanced slowly north seizing Leyviller under smoke cover of the Mortar Platoon, 15th Tank Battalion. By 1400 the town was occupied against little resistance, but direct fire from enemy anti-tank weapons from the north west had forced the tankers to run a gauntlet of fire as they entered the town. Supporting artillery soon silenced the enemy guns. The only impediment Lagrew's force met up to this point was two large craters along the route of advance which were filled in by the engineers. Two platoons of B Company, 50th Armored Infantry Battalion, in an attempt to bypass a shell crater before entering the town, became bogged down in the morass and had to be towed out.

'The move of Lagrew's north column had been slowed, but by 1430 it was through the town and in position to envelop St Jean-Rohrbach from the north along with York's column moving east from Diffembach-les-Hellimer.

'In order to protect Lagrew's north column's flank, Wall moved his Task Force north to Leyviller and made contact with Lagrew and outposted the town that evening while other elements of the 50th Armored Infantry Battalion were sent toward Altrippe to secure the rear.

'After leaving Leyviller, the terrain became suitable for off-road movement and Lagrew employed his tanks astride the road, reinforced by the assault guns. The three infantry companies, 2nd Battalion, 137th Infantry, drew up in close support and the attack progressed toward the strategically located town of St Jean-Rohrbach, the objective of TF Lagrew.

'As the point tank drew up to St Jean-Rohrbach and began deploying into the town, it was immediately knocked out. Lagrew in turn quickly positioned his tanks around the town and started firing as the doughs from 2nd Battalion stormed the objective. The attacking force soon learned that from the west between St Jean-Rohrbach and Diffembach-les-Hellimer York's south column was pinching out several enemy tanks, anti-tank guns, and infantry. The Germans were caught between the two forces. As the German armor began to escape across country, Lagrew's tanks and tank destroyers opened up, scoring hits on two Pz IV's and one tank hunter. At the same time, German infantry was seen withdrawing to the south and every available gun was brought to bear on them; but it was dusk and the extent of German casualties was not determined.'

The fourth short extract from *The Super Sixth* concerns the Sixth Armored's operations in the area of Le Mont de Cadenbronn.

'Diebling was next. The infantry mounted the Shermans from A Company, 68th Tank Battalion, and hit the town against practically no resistance. The only problem encountered was the wayward armored infantry from TF Brown and tanks from C Company, 68th Tank Battalion, who unexpectedly left their zone of advance and entered Diebling and temporarily held up TF Wall.

'By noon Wall reported to Hines that his force was mopping up the town and preparing to move against Metzing directly south of Mont de Cadenbronn. The platoon of tank destroyers from the 603rd moved to the high ground northeast of Diebling and laid a concentration of direct fire on Metzing, while the tankers from A Company were told to look out for German rocket teams that were reported operating from the ditches along the road to Metzing. The infantry again mounted the Shermans and moved east. It was late in the afternoon and suddenly the Germans opened up. Just before the lead tank hit the outskirts of Metzing, the inevitable occurred; a German 88 mm round came crashing into Lieutenant Donald A. Kratzer's tank instantly killing the driver, T/4 Charles R. Shuk, and hitting crewman, Kovalaski, knocking him against Howard McNeill. Kratzer gave the order to bail out and both tankers hit the hatch at the same time, but only one could fit through. McNeill dropped back and Kovalaski scrambled to daylight just as a second round hit on the loaders side, cutting the machine gun in half and completely destroying the radio transmitter and receivers. Though the tank was full of choking smoke and flying shrapnel, four crew members managed to bail out. As the

last man exited the tank the dead driver slumped forward, jamming the throttle to the floor. The smoking tank rolled on in low gear, a dead man at the levers, toward Metzing and finally stopped when it engaged a large tree.

'The fragments caused by the penetration of the German anti-tank round hit the pistol Kovalaski was wearing causing a neat dent. That pistol saved Kovalaski's life. Kratzer, who Read considered one of his better tankers, was quite shaken up but wanted another tank so he could go after the Germans.

'The Germans had opened up on Wall's frontal attack from the heights dominating Metzing. After Kratzer's tank was knocked out, Wall considered the situation precarious because it was close to dusk and he decided that further risk of life was unnecessary. But the problem was that Brown and Davall, operating on Wall's left, continued the attack and were in the process of charging up Mont de Cadenbronn's slopes and getting their tanks picked off by German guns located in the Metzing vicinity. Wall's TF had been instructed to envelop Metzing from the north, but darkness and timidity prevented further operations. As a result, the task force withdrew and proceeded to outpost the area east of Diebling for the night.

'The 212th Armored Field Artillery Battalion, which was in direct support of Wall's force, fired 1750 rounds against enemy anti-aircraft positions, machine gun and artillery positions, troops on the roads and in the woods, and on the towns held by the Germans. But on one occasion the artillerymen fired into a town penetrated by Davall's tankers causing Davall to scream over the radio that those artillerymen "couldn't hit the side of a barn – so stop firing." But fire was continued in general support of the task forces on known German troop concentrations and installations.

'Another important operation occurred on 4 December, when a third task force was ordered to attack and capture Loupershouse on the right flank of TF Wall. Grow wanted Hines to enlarge his front. Task Force Kennedy, which consistuted part of Hines' reserves (69th Tank Battalion and a company of the 9th Armored Infantry Battalion), jumped off at approximately 0830 following a heavy artillery, assault gun, and tank fire concentration. The attack was diversionary to Brown's and Wall's main effort. Nonetheless, it was quite successful when the infantry supported by the assault gun platoon, 69th Tank Battalion, deployed and advanced across the flooded valley and stream under enemy fire and enveloped the town from the south and seized the bridgehead across the Mutterbach River. From there they seized and held the high ground east and south of the town. In short order the 25th Engineers moved in and commenced building a new bridge which was completed before midnight.

'Overall the attack, though somewhat delayed early in the morning due to numerous vehicles bogged down on the approach, nearly carried the objective. One more day would be needed. The general plan for 5 December called for the 44th Armored Infantry Battalion to hold the line along the northeast of Hines' Combat Command, maintaining contact with the 80th Infantry Division to the north west. Briton's TF from Hines' reserves (9th Armored Infantry Battalion and C Company, 68th Tank Battalion; D Company, 69th Tank Battalion; plus units from 603rd Tank Destroyer Battalion and engineers) would continue to the northeast to take the high ground north of Cadenbronn as well as the town of Rouhling. Wall's force was to continue to operate against Metzing and move east toward Ippling along route N 410.

'During the morning of 5 December, TF Wall resumed the attack enveloping Metzing with two forces. Company C, 50th Armored Infantry Battalion, moved directly against the town, while A Company attacked from the north after a short encircling march. The swift maneuver proved too fluid for the German defenders whose resistance melted away, leaving cleaning up and consolidating positions as the only problems.

'Next was the town of Hundling which A Company captured without opposition. Again an envelopment from the north proved successful. In conjunction with the attack against Hundling, forces of TF Wall enveloped Ippling from the north, occupying and cleaning out the town. The operations of Wall's force was much more successful on 5 December because of the employment of the envelopment maneuver as opposed to the direct approach utilized against Metzing on 4 December. Also, the fact that Davall's tanks raced up the slopes late on 4 December placed the German defenses in Metzing in the precarious position of being outflanked, thus alleviating the pressure on Wall's front.

'After completing operations on 5 December, Wall withdrew to the high ground north of Ippling and Hundling for the night.

'Britton's attack on 5 December started shortly after Wall launched his attack against Metzing. A tank-infantry force effected a passage through the lines of TF Brown, picking up elements from the 603rd Tank Destroyer Battalion, and launched an envelopment from the north on the town of Cadenbronn, the vertex of the slopes. By 1100 Britton reported to Hines that the town was captured and the task force was moving east along the high ground in an attempt to envelop the town of Rouhling. By dusk the operation was completed.

'At the end of the day Hines' task forces were on commanding ground above the Sarre River staring into Germany and the Siegfried Line. Grow considered Hines' operation on the 4th and 5 December "one of his best executions." The objective was seized through the successful envelopment of enemy positions. All that was left was to move down the slopes to the bank of the Sarre River and cross into Germany.'

Finally, to round off this series of extracts from the history of Sixth Armored Division, is a quotation concerning a questionnaire which General Bob Grow had to complete on his armoured fighting vehicles. It provides an interesting comment about the Sherman and its crew:

'During the end of the Lorraine Campaign, Grow prepared a reply to a XII Corps questionnaire on tanks. It was the feeling that the Third Army fought the Lorraine Campaign with obsolescent tanks. The best German tanks, the Pz IV and the Panther, outgunned the short barreled 75 mm gun found on the American medium tank, M4. Grow preferred the uparmored Sherman M4A3E2 with the 76 mm high velocity gun for work against armor and concrete bunkers. Also, he recommended one third of the mediums to be armed with 105 howitzers and the remaining two thirds with 76 mm guns. Though the Sherman M4 on a one-to-one basis was inferior to the German tanks (Pz IV, Panther, and Tiger I), it possessed greater maneuverability than the German tanks, and its gyrostabilizer and power traverse were more efficient. But most important and one of the deciding factors was the ability to field a greater number of tanks than the Germans could. In fact if a tank was disabled and the crew left intact, they merely went to the rear to pick up a new vehicle. The American soldier was fortunate; he could depend upon a tremendous amount of material support as compared to his German counterpart, who usually fought against superior material and human odds.'

IMPROVEMENTS TO THE DESIGN

As the Sherman began to be used in action by tank crews all over the world, so ideas for improving its performance came in from the theatres of operations and were passed back to Armored Forces Headquarters for evaluation. Some, of course, resulted in local modifications that could be done in the field and were perhaps appropriate only to a particular theatre or to a particular set of combat circumstances (eg, the Culin hedgerow cutter, as used in the bocage countryside of Normandy), while others were far more major in their scope and required fundamental changes to the basic tank. These improvements can best be described under the three main characteristics of any tank, namely firepower, protection and mobility. Proposed improvements did not just come from the combat users – indeed, even before the first production Shermans had left the assembly line, work had already started at Aberdeen Proving Ground on the design of a modified M4, incorporating improved protection and mobility. APG submitted layout drawings to the Office of the Chief of Ordnance in March 1942. These proposals were for a modified Sherman, some eight tons heavier, with a power-to-weight ratio of 15.3 hp/ton and a top speed of some 35 mph. The new tank had wider tracks to reduce the ground pressure to 10 psi (compared with 13.7 psi for the original M4). Different types of main armament (75 mm, 3-inch or 105 mm howitzer) could be fitted into the same turret by means of interchangeable front plates. There were both good and bad ideas in the new designs, but in fact they were never brought to fruition, although some features of the new project were incorporated into late-production Shermans, so the design work was not completely wasted.

FIREPOWER

Undoubtedly the Sherman was basically a well-designed tank and could hold its own against the early models of enemy medium tanks, such as PzKpfw III and IV. The trouble was, that while the German tanks and tank guns improved and got larger the Sherman remained basically the same. All too often the crews found themselves up against German tanks such as the Tiger and Panther which completely outclassed the M4. In addition, the Germans began to produce PzKpfw III and IV 'Specials', mounting much better guns, with considerably higher muzzle velocity and better penetrative power than the 75 mm on either the Grant or Sherman. American casualties were mainly sustained in frontal attacks against enemy armour, when their lack of lethal gun range meant that the enemy could knock them out at ranges where the standard 75 mm tank gun was useless. However, action reports were not always bad news. The gun control equipment and power traverse of the Sherman were superior to those of the hand-traversed German turrets, so that four or five rounds could be fired before the enemy was able to bring his gun to bear. This superiority combined with the far better manoeuvrability of Shermans over their heavier and more cumbersome opponents did, on occasions, more than even the score, but it has to be said that for the most part the American tanks were outgunned.

The new 76 mm gun M1 seen here in the M34A1 combination gun mount. In an effort to balance the long gun, weights have been welded on to the recoil shield.

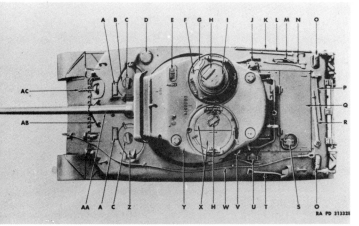

Top view of the M4A1
tank with the 76 mm gun
fitted (Tank Museum).

Having personally seen an entire regiment of Shermans which had been knocked out by one well positioned Jagdtiger, the lesson is inescapable.

As soon as the events of North Africa had indicated the need for a better gun than the 75 mm, Ordnance engineers began work on such a weapon. If it was going to be introduced quickly then it would have to fit into the Sherman without any major alterations, and ideally be able to fire an existing type of ammunition. As the Ordnance history explains, this was exactly the story of the development of the 76 mm tank gun: '... If the new cannon were to reach the battlefield quickly and in quantity, it would have to fit into the tank without major modifications to the turret or mounts and at the same time obviate need for the lengthy process of developing new ammunition. Taking the existing three-inch armor-piercing round as their starting point, Ordnance engineers designed around it a new high-velocity weapon made of high quality steel. The whole development process was incredibly short. The project was initiated on 20 August 1942 and the completed gun, designated the 76 mm M1, was standardised on 10 September, less than a month later. That same autumn, 80 of the new guns were produced and ready for installation.'

The new 76 mm gun weighed only about 300 lb more than the 75 mm, but had a muzzle velocity 600 fps higher when firing AP ammunition and 1,300 fps higher firing HE ammunition. The urgent need for the new weapon was proven, but unfortunately efforts to get it into service quickly were thwarted. First the Armored Force recommended that quantity

production be deferred until they had thoroughly tested several pilot models and determined their tactical suitability. The Ordnance Department was therefore instructed to limit procurement to just 12 Sherman tanks mounting the 76 mm gun, rather than producing the large quantity of new guns required for re-equipment. The Armored Force did not like the turret arrangement, mainly because of lack of space. The heavier gun and longer barrel badly unbalanced the turret and made it very difficult to traverse on a slope. A counterweight at the rear was proposed and the 12 M4A1(76M1)s which had been built in the autumn of 1942 did not begin testing until the following Spring. They were then rejected by the Armored Force, on the grounds that the turret was of a rushed design with insufficient space for proper crew working. This led to the design of a new cast turret – it was actually a pre-production version of the turret designed for the T20/T23 medium tank which was to be the successor to the Sherman. The new model, designated the M4E6, had other good features in addition to giving more space and a better gun mounting for the 76 mm, which included safer ammunition stowage through use of water-jacketed ammunition racks. Unfortunately however, this all seriously delayed the process of getting the new gun into service, so the first production tanks, equipped with the

76 mm gun, were not completed until January 1944.

Although the new gun was a definite improvement upon the 75 mm, in that it could penetrate about an inch more armour than its predecessor, its HE projectile was actually not as effective as that of the 75 mm, and more worrying, it still could not penetrate the frontal armour of either Tiger or Panther. Soon after D-Day, some 138 Shermans equipped with the new gun were sent to Normandy, with disappointing results. 'You mean our 76 won't knock these Panthers out?' General Eisenhower is reported to have asked angrily, in a conversation with General Omar Bradley. 'I thought it was going to be the wonder gun of the war.' 'Oh, it's better than the 75', replied Bradley, 'but the new charge is much too small. She just hasn't the kick to carry her through the German armor.' Ike shook his head and swore. 'Why is it that I am always the last to

hear about this stuff. Ordnance told me this 76 would take care of anything the Germans had. Now I find you can't knock out a damn thing with it.'[21]

Colonel Owsley C. Costlow of Louisville, Kentucky, who was a company commander in 12th Armored Division in north-west Europe, had a better opinion of the 76 mm than his Supreme Commander. He told me: 'Upon approaching a small town, usually just a few stone houses on either side of the road, and not knowing when or where the retreating troops would decide to make their temporary stand, if there was any sign of resistance we would fire one round of 76 mm solid shot into the first house on each side of the road. We found if anyone was in there, they quickly came out and with their hands up. The shot usually penetrated two or more houses; it might go through a picture on one wall, perhaps a desk on another, then on to the next house where it

An M4A3E8, mounting the new 76 mm gun – the M1A2 version fitted with a muzzle brake, which deflected the gases to the side and thus cut down the obscuration caused by dust kicked up by the blast. This tank was called *Blockbuster 3rd* and was commanded by Captain (later Colonel) James H. Leach, CO Co B 37th Tank Battalion, 4th Armored Division (Colonel J. Leach).

would go through a chair on the first wall and a sofa on the other side. I imagine seeing a hole appear on one of your walls, a red streak dashing through your living room, only to go out through the opposite wall would be enough to cause someone, especially a civilian, to give up and come outside ... Of course, if we suspected German soldiers were in the house, we followed the shot with an HE round into the same hole. That could really clean house and also rearrange a good size room.

'On our drive to "liberate" Ansbach, Germany, we began the day at dawn moving quickly through several small villages all without incident. At about the third village, I began to feel uneasy, something wasn't right, everything was too easy, too routine; I felt sure we were being set up for an ambush. Therefore I began to watch the hills and the church bell towers more carefully because we had found if someone was observing us and passing on the information from one town to another, they sometimes signalled from one high place to another. The little villages were within sight of each other all down the narrow valley road. So, seeing some movement in the church steeple in the next town, I had my gunner place a 76 mm HE round in the bell tower. A perfect shot! We had been told that the 76 was more accurate than the 75 but really hadn't seen that much difference except on this shot. He placed it in the bell tower opening at about 800 yards, never hitting the outside wall at all, but it really rang those bells!'

THE FIREFLY

Much later on in the war a high velocity AP round was perfected for the 76 mm, which boosted the muzzle velocity to 3,400 fps – the HVAP M93 Shot (APCR-T), but this would still not penetrate the frontal armour of the Panther at over 300 yards' range. However, there was still one type of Sherman which did mount a gun capable of dealing with the heavy German tanks, this being the British version, the Firefly, mounting the high-velocity 17-pdr gun. This gun had proved its worth as a towed anti-tank gun in the Western Desert, but it had always been intended for use as both a tank and anti-tank gun; indeed, a development of the Cromwell mounting the 17-pdr – designated as the A30 Challenger – was put into production in slow time in December 1943. There were many production problems with Challenger, only small numbers of which were ever produced and these did not reach units until after D-Day. At the same time as the Challenger was

This Sherman IC, also known by the British as the Firefly, mounted the lethal 17-pdr gun, giving it comparable firepower to a Panther. Note the odd location for a stowage box on the front of this tank which was photographed in Normandy (Tank Museum).

being designed, investigations were proceeding on whether the 17-pdr could be mounted in the Sherman into the standard 75 mm turret. [22] Despite some problems, the first pilot conversion was ready by November 1943 and proved highly successful. It was therefore decided to switch production effort away from the Challenger on to producing the Sherman Firefly. Thus, the upgraded tank was available for D-Day on the basis of one per troop, it being the only British tank capable of taking on Tiger or Panther with some expectation of success. Later in the war, Fireflies became more plentiful and were also evaluated by the Americans who would have liked to have obtained 17-pdrs for their Shermans. However British Ordnance was already swamped with British orders so this could not be done, while combat units could ill-afford to send back their tanks for re-gunning. There were three models of the Firefly, these being: Sherman IIC (Firefly) – M4A1 with 17-pdr gun; Sherman IVC (Firefly) – M4A3 with 17-pdr gun; Sherman VC (Firefly) – M4A4 with 17-pdr. See the adjacent table for brief details of the weapon system.

Undoubtedly the Firefly became the 'Sunday Punch' of tank troops lucky enough to have one and was used most successfully against enemy armour. However, one must not get things out of proportion since, despite its excellent gun, the Firefly was still never a true match for the Panther or Tiger, as it lacked the protection which the thicker armour gave the German tanks.

Douglas Gardner of Gloucester was a wireless operator/loader in a Firefly belonging to the Nottinghamshire Yeomanry. He told me: 'The performance of the Firefly was in no way affected through a larger gun, care however had to be taken when manoeuvring round corners in narrow streets as the length of the barrel required gunner and driver to have good liaison to enable turret traverse and tank turning radius to be co-ordinated in order to avoid the gun colliding with buildings and upsetting the fine alignment between gun and sight which were essential for accurate shooting. From my own point of view, as operator/loader, the great advantage was in the provision of a turret hatch; this enabled me to look out and thereby augment the commander's observation. Closed down the Sherman's fighting efficiency was drastically reduced, as were all tanks of those days, and in Normandy most commanders preferred vision

17-PDR GUN MK IV OR VII IN MOUNT No 2 MK 1

Elevation (manual): $+20°$ to $-5°$
Traverse (hydraulic and manual): 15 seconds for one complete revolution
Firing rate (max): 10 rounds/minute
Loading system: manual
Stabiliser: none

Ammunition (77 rounds carried)	Muzzle velocity	Max effective range
APCBC Mk VIII T Shot (APCBC-T)	2,900 fps	2,500 yd
SVDS Shot (APDS-T)	3,950 fps	1,800 yd
HE Mk I – Shell (HE-T)	2,950 fps	12,000 yd

Penetration performance, at $30°$ obliquity

	500 yd	1,000 yd	1,500 yd	2,000 yd
APCBC	5.5 in	5.1 in	4.7 in	4.4 in
SVDS	8.2 in	7.6 in	6.9 in	6.3 in

to safety and fought with head out of hatch. When the commander was wounded I was able to take command, extricate the tank from action and get the commander to first aid, thanks to all-round vision. After the 75 mm, the Firefly muzzle flash and blast proved disturbing, as initially this prevented commander and gunner observing the strike of AP shot, as the velocity was also faster. To obviate this we constantly tested and adjusted gun and sight and tried to get a hit first shot, especially at short range where the blast problem was acute.

'After bitter fighting in the beach-head in Normandy we took part in Operation TOTALISE, the breakout towards Falaise. I would imagine this would have been the largest use of the Sherman en masse; with two columns, each comprising over 200 Shermans, with Priests carrying infantry in the centre, nose to tail, side by side, we advanced by night through the main heavily defended German lines. This difficult and dangerous operation caused heavy losses but was successful in initiating the pincer movements in the Falaise Gap. During the night our Firefly knocked out two enemy tanks and more in the daylight battles; over 20 German tanks were destroyed and I recall when firing the Browning at the infantry advancing among the waist-high corn, I fed so many belts of .30 through it without stopping, that parts of the gun were transparent with heat. We fired at a Tiger at close range and, as the gun fired, I immediately reloaded, the gunner kept his finger on the trigger and as soon as the breech closed it fired again. Examination later showed that both shots went through the same hole, but as usual the Tiger did not brew up. Without doubt the Sherman Firefly was the best Allied tank of World War Two.'

105 mm HOWITZER

The original Sherman design concept had included a 105 mm howitzer version and work began on it in early 1942. Two pilot models of a suitable gun mount were completed by November 1942, being designated as the combination mount M70. They carried the 105 mm howitzer M2A1 together with a coaxial .30 MG. The heavy cast gunshield was some three inches thick. Trials showed that the gun was very difficult to load and that the turret was badly unbalanced, so the howitzer had to be redesigned. Two further pilot models were produced in August 1943, which incorporated all the approved changes (eg, shortened breech block and relocated operating handle for ease of access by the loader, better sighting, increased ammunition stowage, elimination of stabiliser and power traverse, etc).

The redesigned howitzer was designated the 105 mm howitzer M4. Ammunition stowage was increased to 68 rounds (45 in floor racks, 21 in the right sponson and two in the turret ready rack). Brief details of the weapon system are:

The M4E5, mounting the 105 mm howitzer, on test by the Armor Board in August 1943. The .50 MG has been disassembled and stowed on the rear of the turret. Firing a HEAT round, the 105 mm howitzer could penetrate four inches of armour plate.

ADD-ON ARMAMENT

Another way of increasing the Sherman's firepower was to add-on externally some additional type of weapon system, the most favoured being the high explosive rocket. Attachments varied from the somewhat ad hoc British method of roughly fixing a launching rail on the side of the turret, to take a 60 lb aircraft rocket, to far more sophisticated American rocket launchers, such as the T34. Nicknamed 'Calliope', the T34 launcher comprised 60 plastic tubes, each some 7ft 6in long, arranged in banks above the turret as the photograph shows. Calliope fired the 4.5-inch HE rocket and while it was not particularly accurate against point targets it could produce quite devastating results firing in salvoes. Colonel Owsley Costlow had this to say about Calliope:

'Shortly before our drive to the Rhine River, a 60-tube rocket launcher, T34, "Calliope" was added to one of the tanks in the company's Second Platoon. It seems that each of the three medium tank companies in the battalion re-

---

105 MM HOWITZER M4 IN MOUNT M52

Elevation (manual): $+35°$ to $-10°$
Traverse (manual, hydraulic also on later production tanks): 15 seconds for one complete revolution
Firing rate (max): 8 rounds/minute
Loading system: manual
Stabiliser: only on later production tanks

Ammunition (68 rounds carried)	Muzzle velocity	Max range
HE M1 Shell (HE)	1,550 fps	12,205 yd
HEAT M67 Shell (HEAT-T)	1,250 fps	8,590 yd
WP M60 Shell Smoke	1,550 fps	12,150 yd
HC BE M48 Shell Smoke	1,550 fps	12,205 yd

Penetration performance: Homogeneous armour at 0° obliquity, using HEAT M67: 4 in at any range.

ceived one. This was in addition to the bull-dozer blade that had been placed on another second platoon tank. They had all the odd pieces of equipment in their platoon. On 24 March 1945, our reinforced battalion task force prepared to attack Germersheim, France, and seize the bridge there over the Rhine. By this time I was in command of A Company which was to be the fire support for the attack. The other two battalion Calliopes had been brought up during the night so at first light I commanded three 60-tube rocket laun-chers and could deliver 180 rounds of 4.5-inch rockets at a minute's notice. It was almost like being a Division Artillery Commander! How-ever, the rockets were noted for their inaccuracy, with a ratio of at least 10% rounds over and another 10% short, so they could be used only in general fire support against an area target. As the first tanks moved out for the attack, I had one Calliope cover the left flank, another cover the right, and the third to be prepared to fire ahead of the leading tanks into the town, if requested. I believe I was first Calliope fire support commander in the Divi-sion and perhaps in all of Seventh Army.'

Calliope was probably the most widely used of the various types of 4.5-inch rocket laun-chers, but they were not the only type em-ployed. In addition, there were various mount-

**oading 4.5-inch rockets
to the firing tubes of
Calliope.**

ings for 7.2-inch demolition rockets, including versions where the demolition rocket launcher replaced the tank's main armament.

SECONDARY ARMAMENT

There was also a requirement to improve the tank's secondary armament so as to conserve main gun ammunition when dealing with non-armoured targets. The .30 machine-guns were of limited use against anything other than personnel and the bow gun was particularly difficult to aim accurately. The .50 on top was more effective, but to use it one of the crew had to expose himself to enemy fire. Various test rigs were tried out, to mount twin .30s or twin .50s atop the commander's hatch, fired remotely from inside the tank, but none of these mounts ever entered service. Better sighting

was also trialled for the bow gun, with a linkage joining the gun to the bow gunner's periscope, which was fitted with a telescopic sight, but few such modifications were made to in service tanks before the end of the war.

PROTECTION

The 'Tommy Cooker' clearly needed better protection, especially for use in assault operations, when the tank was exposed to heavy and continuous enemy fire. In addition to the US Army requirements, the British estimated that they would need 8,500 heavy assault tanks[23], so there was considerable interest in the new design, designated as the T14. The pilot model of the T14, later called 'Jumbo', weighed in at 47 tons and was completed in July 1943. It had extra wide tracks, a top speed of 24 mph, and

How to protect your
Sherman tank with
sandbags! This cannot
really have been a very
good system, but clearly
the crews felt that it was
worthwhile.

The 'Biggie' that did
make it was the
M4A3E2, nicknamed
'Jumbo'. Its additional
armour increased the
combat weight to about
84,000 lb (a good
10,000 lb heavier than a

normal Sherman). The
assault tanks were used
in Europe with
considerable success.
This one, belonging to
4th Armored Division
has been re-armed with
a 76 mm gun.

was armed with a 75 mm gun, although plans were made to install the 105 mm howitzer. The tank was soon found to have many faults, mobility was poor and it was difficult to maintain, the armoured shields over the suspension making track adjustment very difficult. The project was dropped after only two T14s had been built, the first pilot being shipped to Aberdeen Proving Ground in November 1943 and the other to the UK, where it is still on display at the Tank Museum, Bovington Camp.

Despite the failure of the Jumbo, requirement for better protection still remained. The dangers from short-range anti-tank weapons, such as the German Panzerfaust, were such that there were many local 'modifications' made. Ed Bollard of East Stroudsberg, Pennsylvania, who served in Shermans with the US Marine Corps in the Pacific, told me: 'One of the most ingenious additions to the Sherman was an idea that one of our Warrant Officers developed. In order to provide extra protection he devised a method of attaching large boards (2 by 10s or 2 by 12s) on to the sides by means of large bolts welded to the tank. He would leave a four to six inch gap between the board and the side of the tank. Into this space he would pour concrete. After the battles of Saipan and Iwo Jima, the additions were in tatters. However, to my recollection, we only had one tank pierced and that was on Iwo by a high velocity 47 mm. He also welded extra track blocks on to the front slope plate and all round the turret sides. These not only provided more protection but also gave us extra track blocks, for immediate repairs in the field.'

Official steps were also taken with the demise of the T14 project and it was decided to modify the M4A3 model, by adding armour on to all hull surfaces to give a maximum thickness of four inches. In addition, a new cast turret was designed which had six inch-thick armour on its front, sides and rear. The extra armour put up the weight to about 42 tons which reduced the top speed to 22 mph and had a similar effect upon the tank's cross-country performance. Permanent grousers – known as 'duckbills' – were fitted to the tracks to help improve the performance and a total of 254 of these assault tanks, designated as the M4A3E2, were produced in May/June 1944 and shipped to Europe where they were used in battle and considered by all to be very satisfactory. Other attempts at protection included add-on plastic spaced armour (see photograph).

Another form of protection which was incorporated into the later models was directed at trying to reduce the prevalence of ammunition fires. This was done by the installation of what was called 'wet stowage', which comprised the relocation of all main gun ammunition in water-protected racks located below the turret ring. For example, for the 75 mm gun, there were ten boxes in the hull which held 100 rounds and needed just over 37 gallons of water, while a further one gallon was needed to protect the four ready rounds. The

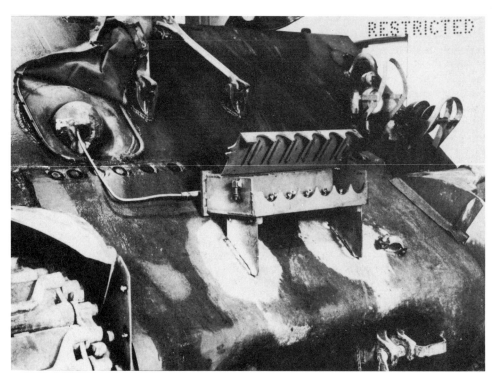

RESTRICTED

One of a trio of anti-personnel devices for use on Sherman was an anti-personnel mine holder fixed on the outside. The others were the Scorpion flame projector and an explosive-loaded pipe. Because of the inherent danger to friendly forces, these devices could only have been used when tanks were operating alone. None saw combat action.

water had to be prevented from freezing in the winter and from corroding the metal containers, so a suitable additive was produced known as 'Ammudamp'.

Finally, various odd devices were tried to protect against close assault by 'Kamikaze' infantry with explosive charges and the like. These devices included the mounting of hand grenades, AP mines, even explosive filled piping on the outside of the tank, while another rather bizarre idea was a bullet deflector to fit on to the end of a .45 sub-machine-gun. The SMG was mounted inside the turret and the deflector outside on top of the turret alongside the periscope. The curved deflector successfully 'bent' the trajectory of the bullet through 90° and trials showed that targets could be effectively engaged some 100 feet away from the tank!

MOBILITY

ENGINE IMPROVEMENTS
The original engine fitted to the M4 was the R975 Wright-Whirlwind nine-cylinder, 400 horsepower radial, which had previously been widely used in training planes and light aircraft. Even when fitted to the medium M3 it had produced problems due to lack of power, while space restrictions made proper cooling and ready access virtually impossible. 'The engine as presently installed, is definitely under-powered. Improvements to this installation have increased the horsepower available but the HP/Wt ratio is still too low to give a completely satisfactory performance.'[24] Although this gave an ideal opportunity to tackle the tank engine problem, it was not the right time as far as world events were concerned, the war could not stop while America sorted out its manufacturing difficulties. As a result, the Ordnance Department had to keep the R975 in spite of its shortcomings. However, despite increased radial engine production, it soon became clear that the use of other different types of power plant would be needed to keep pace with the mushrooming aircraft industry, let alone the tank production. As we have seen, the development of alternate engines went ahead, and while this did not necessarily lead to improved performance, it did enable production targets to be met.

TRANSMISSION AND RUNNING GEAR
Work was done to produce a successful new high-speed reverse transmission which also incorporated a low level oil system, but they

M4 SHERMAN POWERPLANTS

Engine	Type	Work done	Result
Wright-Continental R975 C1 (400 hp at 2,400 rpm)	9-cylinder 4-cycle radial petrol	Radiation area on cylinder heads enlarged, cast aluminium muffs used to increase heat transfer on cylinders; new carburetter fitted; supercharger ratio reduced.	Power output increased to 460 hp. Engine then designated R975 C4 and became standard engine for new production M4s & M4A1s.
General Motors 6046 (twin 6-71) twin in-line diesel. (410 hp at 2,900 rpm)	12-cylinder 2-cycle twin in-line diesel	Initial air cleaner problems were partly solved, engine had good pulling power especially at low speeds. GM also developed another diesel engine the V8-184 (based on a marine diesel) which was rated at 600 hp. Trials took place in 1944–45 with new engine in a M4A2E1.	Performance of new engine greatly exceeded that of standard Sherman, but was never put into production.
Chrysler A 57 (425 hp at 2,850 rpm)	30-cylinder 4-cycle multibank petrol	Produced as an experiment to avert a threatened shortage of air-cooled radials. A 57 was developed in four months. Problems due to size, access and weight (5,400 lb dry as opposed to 1,137 lb for the R975C1) did not prove insurmountable. Early in 1943 Chrysler asked for approval to install a privately-developed water-cooled V12 engine known as the A 65. Fitted to a modified M4A4 with length of hull increased by $9\frac{1}{2}$ in to take new engine.	A 65 produced 580 hp at 2,400 rpm but trial was closed in Nov 1943.
Ford GAA (500 hp at 2,000 rpm)	8-cylinder 4-cycle 60° Vee petrol	The US Army preferred this engine and it was developed to power the successors of Sherman. The low silhouette Ford V8 Model GAN was essentially the same engine as the GAA, but modified to fit into a much lower chassis. Later still the designation was changed to GAF.	GAF engine was used to power the Pershing T26 medium tank.
Ordnance RD 1280 (497 hp at 3,000 rpm)	9-cylinder 4-cycle radial diesel	No actual improvements to RD 1280, however the radial diesel experiments included work on 9- and 18-cylinder, air-cooled, radial diesels made by the Guiberson Diesel Engine Co.	Project only partly completed as engines found to be too bulky for tank installation.

Drawing of the new horizontal volute spring suspension, known either as 'HVSS' or 'Easy Eight' as tanks when fitted with HVSS took the nomenclature 'E8' into their designation (Tank Museum).

were not fitted until after the war.

The major change in running gear came with the introduction of horizontal volute spring suspension (HVSS). Although this type of suspension had been trialled as early as 1942, trials with M4 did not begin until 1943. Tests showed that performance was greatly improved with the new running gear, but there was excessive wear on the tracks (T66), so a new 23-inch double pin steel track (T80) was developed which had a much longer life. The weight of the tank was increased by over $1\frac{1}{3}$ tons with HVSS fitted, and by over two tons with the new tracks as well. However, the wide tracks meant a larger ground contact area so the overall ground pressure was reduced. By mid-1944, HVSS was recommended for all new production M4s.

'Duckbills' (as these track grousers were called) on this M4A3 helped to reduce the ground pressure and made it easier to move across bad going.

OTHER IMPROVEMENTS TO MOBILITY

To improve performance in muddy terrain extended end connectors, or 'duckbills' as they were called, were fitted. Some combat problems demanded on the spot answers – such as the difficulties faced in the bocage country of Normandy, where thick hedgerows on the sides of the narrow sunken roads greatly hindered tank movement. They were just too thick and strong to burst through and a tank became dangerously exposed if it managed to climb over the top. This led to the invention of a hedgerow cutter, nicknamed the 'Rhinoceros' for obvious reasons, as it was made of steel angles which were then welded to the front of the tank forming a tusklike structure. The 'tusk' cut into the base of the hedge and the tank was then able to push its way through, taking part of the hedge along with it and completely burying any enemy with a Panzerfaust who happened to be lurking behind it! The invention was also known as the 'Culin

sts at APG showed
at the maximum size
the grousers was
ins when installed on
ndard tracks,
erwise the tracks
re unstable and could
thrown easily.
wever, with the
SS and 23-inch T60
cks, it was possible to
up to 39 inches as
n here.

ose-up of the Culin
dgerow cutter, which
alt most effectively
th the bocage hedges.

hedgerow cutter' after its inventor, Sergeant G. Culin of the 102nd Cavalry Reconnaissance Squadron who later received the Legion of Merit in recognition of his brainwave. Over 500 tanks were fitted with the Rhinoceros in time for the Normandy breakout, much of the steel used coming from German beach defence obstacles.

FORDING EQUIPMENT

The need to cross all types of obstacles led to the production of various specialised armoured vehicles, some of which were based upon the Sherman and these will be dealt with in the next chapter. However, the ability for every tank to be able to ford water of a reasonable depth was essential in order to get off landing craft on to beaches, or cross some rivers. A waterproofing kit was developed for the Sherman and with it fitted the tank could operate in water about six feet deep. This is how Ed Bollard remembers them:

'Fording kits . . . they were not at all difficult to affix to the tank. They were shaped like a large letter L with the lower part fitting over the rear exhaust area so as to keep the water out of the engine. Then the long vertical line of the L extended several feet into the air permitting the tank to waddle toward the beach in water up to the bottom of the turret. On the side of the tank we had a pick, shovel, axe and sledge attached. When we hit the beach we were accompanied by our recconaissance teams who were on foot. They were all taught to go to each tank as it reached the beach and knock off the fording kit. This was not hard as they were taped on with waterproof tape. If a recon man was not in the area, one of the crew did the job. We left the kits where they fell. Perhaps someone came along later and salvaged them but I doubt it.'

6 SHERMAN VARIANTS

A BEWILDERING ARRAY

The vast number of variants produced from the basic Sherman gun tank almost defies description, as they form such a bewildering array, difficult to encompass in one short chapter. Some, while retaining most of the main components of the medium M4 tank – eg, chassis, turret, power train and running gear – had major additions 'bolted on' so that the resulting AFV could deal with a particular situation, such as being able to swim, clear obstacles, spit fire, etc, but they still retained the shape and style of a gun tank. Others changed so many of their major components as to no longer be able to be called a tank and had to be given another name – in this category I would place self-propelled artillery, tank destroyers and tank recovery vehicles. Some of the variants were fairly conventional, others were so new and so strange as to be deserving the generic title 'Funnies' which the British irreverently called their specialised armour. In the vast army assembled for D-Day, the now famous 79th Armoured Division, commanded by Major General Sir Percy Hobart, contained nothing but specialised AFVs. 'Hobo' was an outstanding, outspoken and controversial figure, already responsible for the training of two of the finest ever armoured divisions, the 7th and the 11th. The basic concept of many of his 'Funnies' came from his own fertile imagination, but of course only a few were based upon the Sherman tank. However, there were large numbers of amphibious Sherman DD gun tanks and Sherman Crab mine clearing tanks in his division, which were employed very successfully during the Normandy landings. It was the work of these AFVs, as part of the assault forces on the British beachheads, which was largely responsible for the success of the British landings. Some of the 'Funnies' remained classified as Top Secret right up to the end of the war. In this chapter we deal first with the Sherman 'Funnies' and then move on to describe in broad terms, the other more conventional variants.

AMPHIBIOUS DEVICES

In planning for the D-Day assault, it had quickly become evident that much would depend upon the Allies being able to get armour ashore to support the leading infantry. This requirement was no different for the US Forces in the Pacific theatre although, while the end product was the same, namely a 'swimming tank', the methods used to make it amphibious were very different.

THE DD TANK

Considerable work had been done in the UK on the use of a highly secret flotation screen system, invented by an emigré Hungarian engineer, Nicholas Straussler, and already used successfully on the British Valentine. However, 'Hobo' was adamant that his DD tanks ('DD' stands for Duplex Drive) would be based upon the current front-line main battle tank, the Sherman, and not the obsolescent Valentine, which was by then no match for the German tank guns. The Sherman DD used a rubberised canvas folding screen, which was mounted on to a mild steel framework, welded on to the tank. As the photographs show, the screen was erected around the fully waterproofed tank, using a series of 36 tubular rubber pillars inflated by compressed air. It took about 15 minutes to erect. The screen was then locked into place with steel struts and remained so until the DD reached the shore and needed to fire its guns. Propulsion was via two 26-inch propellers at the rear, connected to the tracks via a bevel gear and pinion which engaged with sprocket rings attached to the outside of the tank's idlers. A speed of five to six mph was possible in water, while steering was achieved by swivelling the propellers.

For the crews of these secret machines, underwater escape training was a very necessary but alarming experience, as Bernard Cuttiford, late of the Staffordshire Yeomanry recalls: '... One of the most frightening parts of the training as far as I was concerned was the escape training carried out at Gosport sub-

A Sherman DD with th[] screen lowered and the propellers raised for land operation. The Sherman in the photo an M4A2.

Close-up of the tubula[] rubber pillars which were inflated with compressed air, plus t[] locking steel struts (Tank Museum).

marine base, using a large indoor water-tank and a modified version of the Davis submarine escape apparatus, but smaller so that we could get out of the tank hatches. The hull of a tank was in the bottom, and the crew, wearing nothing but denims and plimsolls, plus an escape apparatus, climbed down iron ladders to take up their respective positions in the tank. With each crew member was a Royal Navy frogman, who made sure there was no premature baling out! The cocks were then opened and the whole tank flooded. The water started creeping over my legs, over my lap and up my chest. By this time I had my mouthpiece in and nose clip on the bridge of my nose. When the water reached my chin I found that I was panicking a bit and trying to get out, but without success as there was a great big Navy frogman with his feet on my shoulders keeping me in! So it was nose clip down to close the nose, open valve and start breathing through the mouth, and I found that I was able to breathe under water. The panic subsided a bit and eventually we were allowed up one at a time, guided by our respective frogman. Advanced training was carried out at Scunthorpe where we were taught to handle our craft in tidal waters and choppy seas, day and night, in all weathers, practising navigation, station keeping and compass adjustments. Funny isn't it, I never wanted to be a sailor!'

A total of ten regiments – five British, two Canadian and three American – were trained on DD, eight taking part in the D-Day landings. Here is how Pat Hennessy, then a young Lance Corporal commanding a Sherman DD in the 13th/18th Hussars, remembers the landings: '... June 1st saw us embark at Gosport on to a Landing Craft Tank (LCT) and move out into the Solent. For two days and nights we wallowed about in fairly rough seas waiting for the rest of the armada to assemble. Time and again we cleaned our guns, read endless books and smoked. Many were seasick ... Well before dawn on 6 June we heard the airborne spearhead going in while we checked our guns and underwater apparatus. Then came the order to board tanks and inflate the screens. Everything seemed to work. The screens rose around the tanks and we secured the struts and periscopes. Then the ramp on the LCT was lowered and we could see the shore some 5,000 yards away.

'The first tank off was Sergeant Charlie Rattles of 4th Troop. We followed and as we righted in the water, we could see other tanks launching on both sides of us. There was much noise and smoke and it was quite a struggle to keep the tank on course. Apart from our driver, Trooper Harry Bone, we were all on deck at the time and I vividly remember witnessing the tragedy which befell Captain Noel Denny's tank as it was overtaken and run down by our own LCT. It took us well over an hour to get close to the beach, the sea was rough and the noise increasing. As we felt the tracks grind on the shelving bottom, we dropped our float screen and opened fire on the line of houses which were our targets. We had a quick discussion as to whether we should move on up the beach and chance the mines which had not yet been cleared, but suddenly the problem was solved for us. We had landed on an incoming tide and the water was getting deeper. Then one large wave swamped the engine and that was that!'

Pat Hennessy (recently retired from the RAF with the rank of Group Captain) went on to tell how, after continuing to fire for a while, the tank became so flooded that they had to bale out and make for shore in a rubber dinghy. En route, they were hit and sunk by enemy fire. After more adventures, he and his crew managed to meet up that evening, with the survivors of their squadron who by then had only five serviceable tanks remaining.

Another D-Day veteran, Albert Johnson,

was the wireless operator/loader on a Sherman DD of B Squadron 4th/7th Dragoon Guards, who were supporting the Green Howards in 50th Northumbrian Division. He recalls: 'We had been training in our special role in DD tanks since April 1943 and were due to swim into the beach of La Riviere, four kilometres east of Arromanches, having been launched from the landing craft some 4,000 yards out. Personal equipment included a simplified version of the Davis Escape Apparatus, as a DD tank would sink like a stone if the screen collapsed. We had been on our small landing craft tank over 24 hours on the morning of 6 June, owing to the postponement of D-Day. After a rough time tossing about in heavy seas for hours before the actual crossing most of us were seasick and that didn't do much for morale! It also accounted for my lack of concern when I inadvertently trod on my escape apparatus and bust the valve! That grey dawn was not brightened by the news that the DD tanks would not be launched on our front owing to the heavy swell. We felt our chances

of being hit on the run-in were much higher when still on the LCT.

'As the sun came up an amazing sight met our eyes. The sea was full of ships as far as we could see, of all shapes and sizes. Spirits began to rise and when the naval bombardment opened up we felt we couldn't fail as the explosions could be clearly seen on the low-lying shore ahead. I remember in particular one destroyer or frigate equipped with rocket launchers firing from our rear. It seemed to be very accurate as we could see the bursts run along the beach. However, one battery of six or so kept dropping the odd rocket among the infantry landing craft ahead of us.

'We went straight into the beach and as the LCT grounded, down came the door. The tank's DD screen was erect and all but the tank commander with his periscope were temporarily blind. There was a certain amount of wading to do and it was a matter of fine judgment for the troop leader deciding when to drop the screen. The time was around 7.30 am and after interminable seconds the order came

Good shot of a DD entering the water. This photo was taken in the Neckar River sector in Germany, 13 April 1945 and shows a DDI (this type had an extended rear screen and modified locking struts) belonging to 781st Tank Battalion.

but the screen stuck partially up. To traverse the turret the screen had to be down and I got the order to get out and clear it. As I did so a mortar shell fell on the other side of the tank. I moved rather smartish to pull the screen down and remount!

'The tide was still out and all the beach obstacles, ramps and tetrahedra were exposed to view. All we had to do was weave about in-between them. We followed a mine-clearing flail tank of the Westminster Dragoons up and off the beach. We even crossed an anti-tank ditch before the Germans had time to blow it. In what seemed a very short time we headed inland down a lane which passed close to the Mont Fleury battery of heavy guns which could have dominated everything at sea from Arromanches eastwards had it not been destroyed by HMS *Belfast*.

'I didn't know that at the time but was enjoying myself with my head out of the turret viewing the exciting events! [DD Shermans had two hatches in the turret.] The Green Howards were going ahead in long files on both sides of the land and at the high port. Suddenly the low branch of a tree appeared to my front and as I ducked I mistakenly fired a burst of Browning, fortunately, over the heads of our infantry. Minutes later the gunner stretched his legs and hit the 75 mm gun button and boom went an inadvertent shot of HE dead ahead. To say the least the Troop Leader wasn't very pleased with us. By the time a burst of Spandau carried away our turret top mounted Browning I'd had enough "viewing" for the day.

'For the rest of the day my Troop of tanks had a fine time charging across country and firing at anything that moved. We were now ahead of the Green Howards and only hoped that they had carriers and some transport to keep up with us. We reached Villiers-le-Sec four kilometres inland without trouble. However, having crossed the River Seulles the Squadron ran into opposition at St Gabriel and had one tank knocked out. I remember seeing the driver and co-driver walking back having escaped via the hatch in the tank floor. Only later did I learn that my best friend had been badly wounded. We pushed on to the area of Brecy nearly six miles inland. As the light faded I could see another of our tanks on fire. As the action died out I switched the tank wireless over to the nine o'clock news from London. We slept well that night under the tank tarpaulin.'

Before leaving DD tanks, mention must be made of another gadget that went by the improbable name of 'Belch' and yet another called 'Ginandit'. The former was a means of protecting the DD screen from fire damage caused, for example, by burning oil on the water. It consisted of a small petrol engine driving a pump which pumped up sea water to a series of jets placed around the top of the screen – it worked most satisfactorily. 'Ginandit' was a type of folded mat, which was mounted on a rack above the tank and could be projected in front when the vehicle had to climb up mud banks, etc, during river crossings. The mat gave better traction. Finally, there was a light armoured cover designed to protect the folded DD screen from small arms fire and other damage called 'Topee'.

OTHER FLOTATION GEAR

After the Normandy operations the DDs were used for various river crossings, the most important being on the Rhine in March 1945. The US Army Ordnance did not like the DD tank, considering it to be unseaworthy and dangerous. They also did not like the fact that the tank could not use its guns when afloat. Instead they favoured various types of compartmented, plastic-filled, steel floats which were attached to the front, rear and sides, to give buoyancy. Propulsion was via the moving tracks and two large rudders at the rear steered the tank – via ropes to the commander. The most successful of these was the T6 which was later standardised as the M19. The M19s were used during the invasion of Okinawa in April 1945, some landing successfully, while others struck reefs which surrounded the beaches and holed their long floats. Fully waterproofed tanks, that could be landed directly on the reefs and then wade ashore on to the beach, eventually proved more successful than the rather cumbersome flotation gear.

Below. A good photograph of the US T6 swimming device which the Ordnance Department preferred to DD screens. Compartmented steel floats, filled with plastic foam and waterproofed, were attached to the front, rear and sides of the tank. The rudders at the rear were controlled by ropes from the turret. The M4A1 in the photograph was on the shore of Bougainville in October 1944.

Above. Deep fording equipment fitted to this USMC Sherman as it comes ashore on Tinan, July 1944. Properly waterproofed with this kit a Sherman could operate in water up to about six feet deep. There were similar kits for other types of tank and AFVs (USMC).

ENGINEER VEHICLES

TANK DOZERS

These originated from the requirement to be able to bulldoze while under enemy fire, so that such tasks as clearing roads, filling in bomb and shell craters, etc, could be done even when the enemy was engaging the area of operations with direct fire. There was also another interesting use for the armoured bulldozer and that was to deal with fires in ammunition dumps, which had been found to be a considerable hazard, particularly in the very constricted Anzio area in Italy, where a fire was started in one or other of the ammunition dumps nearly every night by enemy shelling. Initially the fires were fought using hand shovels and dirt, but later some 40-gallon foamite fire extinguishers were mounted on half-tracks so that they could be got closer to the blaze. However, it was the tank dozer that really saved the day. Fighting fires with ordinary tanks had been tried in Tunisia, but at Anzio, the VI Corps ammunition officer, Major John Merrill, suggested putting a bulldozer blade on the front of a tank and in April 1944, 197th Ordnance Battalion at Capua got bulldozer blades from the Engineers and welded them on to some M4 tanks and T2 tank recovery vehicles. Four

were shipped to Anzio and distributed among the hardest hit ammunition dumps, where they were an immediate success. They were able to quickly smother fires with dirt, extinguishing them far faster and more effectively than ever before. In May, proper Engineer conversion kits for installing bulldozer blades on M4 tanks were obtained from the States, the kits having been initially designed with a mine clearing role in view.

Tank dozers, based upon the M4, were used in most theatres, nearly 2,000 conversion kits – designated as the Bulldozer, Tank Mounting, M1 – being produced before the end of hostilities. There were also a number of other models of mounting kits, as the photographs show, and armoured bulldozers did sterling work everywhere, especially in the jungles and other difficult terrain. Sadly, their use on the D-Day beaches was very curtailed, as only six of the original sixteen dozers due to land on Omaha beach reached the shore safely and one of those had lost its blade. These armoured dozers were in fact substituting on the US beaches for the AVRE (Armoured Vehicle, Royal Engineers) which did such a marvellous job on the British beaches, and their loss was a major factor in the heavy casualties suffered by US Army combat engineers on D-Day.

ank dozer in action in rance. The tank-mounted bulldozer M1 seen here; note the moured cover behind e centre of the blade hich was to protect the ydraulic jack which oved the blade.

ARMOURED ENGINEER VEHICLES

The British AVRE was, of course, based upon the Churchill tank and the US Army decided to develop a similar vehicle based upon the Sherman. The first test vehicles had their main armament removed, together with ammunition racks and other internal storage. Double doors of one inch thick armour plate were fitted on the front of the turret, a second side door fitted in the left-hand sponson, while hand rails and an attachment to take a dozer blade were fitted to the outside of the tank. One of the pilot models was also equipped with the 7.2-inch T2 rocket launcher located above the turret. Tests showed that the turret doors were both vulnerable and difficult to use, so they were replaced by a steel plug, with the gunshield and gunmount left in place. Also the T40 launcher was substituted for the T2. It was envisaged that the AEV would have a crew of six men and carry a 1,000 lb load of explosive, which was then hand placed as necessary by a team of three outside and one inside tossing out the explosives. Other items trialled were an armoured trailer which could carry a further 2,200 lb of explosives, toboggan-type pallets, charge placers, mine ploughs, demolition snakes (explosive-filled hoses) and other engineer equipment. Armament for the vehicle comprised the .30 bow MG, plus an 81 mm mortar which could be fired out of the turret hatch. 100 conversion kits were authorised, but only two vehicles were ever prepared and crewed by the time the war finished. The US Army thus made no combat use of any type of armoured engineer vehicle.

Other trials were centred around producing a tank with a suitable demolition gun (cf; the 12-inch spigot mortar on the British AVRE

which could throw its 25 lb HE charge – known as the 'Flying Dustbin' – some 80 yards with considerable accuracy) and another turret-mounted 7.2-inch rocket launcher was trialled in place of the tank's main armament. Finally, the T31 demolition tank was planned, which had two T94 7.2-inch rocket launchers mounted one on each side of a thin turret in which was located two .30 MGs in ball mountings, with a dummy howitzer barrel in between them. The rocket launchers were of the revolver type, each carrying five rockets, with a further 20 available for reloading, which could be achieved internally. On the hull there were fittings to attach a bulldozer unit (M1A1), plus a 50-gallon flame thrower unit in the right sponson. A periscopic flame gun could be fitted into either the assistant driver's hatch or the commander's cupola, while the standard bow MG was retained. Only one pilot demolition tank was ever built and this had difficulties with the operation of the rocket launchers. The project was cancelled in January 1946. The

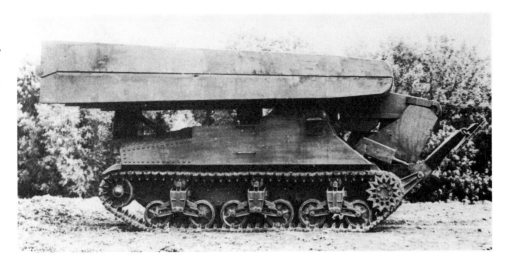

only other engineer conversions of the M4 were ad hoc ones, for example, to carry portable bridges or fascines, as the photographs show.

FLAME THROWERS

The US Army showed only a passing interest in the tank-mounted flame throwers, until the effectiveness of flame against Japanese bunkers and strongpoints was demonstrated at Guadacanal in January 1943, where the first portable flame throwers were used. Trials had taken place, just prior to World War Two, into the feasibility of mounting a flame thrower on to a medium tank, with the E2 flame gun being installed in the turret of the M2 medium. Later, in 1942, the E3 flame gun had been successfully tried in the turret of the M3 medium, replacing the 37 mm gun; however, it

A bow gun mount flame thrower lights up the gloom of the Hurtgen Forest, Germany, during the drive towards the Roer River by First Army troops. Fuel was propelled by compressed air at 350–375 psi operating pressure.

did not see active service. It took nearly another three years before tank-mounted flame throwers saw action in the Pacific theatre, when the Chemical Warfare Service installed Canadian flame guns into some old M3A1 light tanks. Called the 'Satan', it was used so successfully by the US Marine Corps at Saipan and Tinan, for tackling the stubborn enemy in dugouts, canefields, buildings and caves, that the Tenth Army requested that large capacity flame throwers be installed on Sherman medium tanks.[25] On the other side of the world, the British were considerably further ahead in the use of flame and the Crocodile – a Churchill tank equipped with a flame gun in place of its bow machine-gun and towing a trailer of flame fluid – formed an integral part of 79th Armoured Division and was used to great effect from D-Day onwards. Crocodiles were still in service after the war ended, C Squadron 7th Royal Tank Regiment being so equipped when they went to fight for the United Nations in the Korean War in 1950.

In World War Two only the US Marines Corps ever had any main armament flame guns, mounted in the barrels of their M4s' 75 mm gun. They were used in Okinawa, where according to General Richardson[26] they were 'of incalculable value. In fact the Infantry

and the Marines came to rely on this weapon of warfare as their greatest support.' Ed Bollard, late USMC again: 'Flame throwers. I never saw any fitted into the hull, and since I was in the Shermans from the beginning to the end, I would say that we never had this type of mount. Our flame throwers all were fired down the barrel of the 75 mm gun that each tank mounted. We found out later that this was particularly distressing to the Japs as they never knew which of the tanks carried flame and which carried regular ammo. That only added to their great fear of the tanks . . . We had

A Sherman M4A2, belonging to the USMC firing its main armament flame thrower POS-CWS '75' H-1, during fighting in Okinawa in March 1945 As Ed Bollard testifies they were extremely effective.

T33 flame thrower tank, which was based on an M4A3E2, the heavily armoured assault tank. Note that the bow machine-gun mount has been eliminated. Alongside the lightweight 75 mm gun M6 (main armament) was the E20-20 flame thrower, which had its own separate shield. An auxiliary E21 flame gun was to be mounted in the periscope holder of the tank commander's cupola which could be traversed through 240° to the sides and rear, thus providing close-in protection. In fact when the pilot model of the T33 was built, an E124 periscopic flame gun was substituted. Work on the T33 continued after the war up to June 1948, but no further models were built other than the three pilots.

a tube that fitted into the barrel of the 75 mm gun. Inside the tank we had two cylinders. The one carried napalm which we pumped up into the barrel. The other contained carbon dioxide which compressed the napalm and under pressure fired it. We had an igniter at the end of the gun barrel which would spark the charge as it emerged from the end of the barrel ... this was truly a powerful weapon, if you can imagine a 30-ton tank rolling toward you spewing a mass of flames plus heavy fire from two machine guns ...

'I believe that the flame throwers were the weapon that the Japs hated the most. They were effective in attacking pillboxes, bunkers and caves. Iwo was loaded with caves. We could fire this flame up to a distance of 100 yards and it was quite accurate. You didn't have to hit the enemy to kill him, merely firing into the mouth of a cave would suck out the oxygen in a matter of seconds and suffocate all within.'

MINE CLEARING DEVICES

THE FLAILS
Once ashore on an enemy beach it was fully expected that the armour would find its way forward blocked by extensive enemy minefields. This had happened before, for example in the desert battles of El Alamein, and clearly a rapid and effective method of getting through such obstacles was essential. To date, prodding and hand-lifting of mines had provided the only satisfactory answer, although some rudimentary mechanical means had been tried with limited success. In the desert this had centred upon a type of rotor flail, comprising a large rotating cylinder fixed in front of a tank, to which were attached a series of heavy chains. When the drum was rotated, the chains swung through the air and

A Sherman Crab flail, the most successful type of mine clearing device used in the war. This one was photographed at Warminster, Wiltshire in 1948 and belonged to 3 RTR (P. Burrell).

beat on the ground, hopefully detonating any mine they struck. The British progressed with the flail principle and adapted various types of mine exploder equipments to fit on to the Sherman tank, including the Scorpion, Marquis, Lobster and Crab (see photograph). The last named of these was undoubtedly the most successful type of mechanical mine clearing device used in World War Two. It was simple, rugged and had the big advantage of not unduly affecting the use of the tank's main armament except to restrict its arc of fire. The flail rotor projected on two arms in front of the tank and was driven by the main engine, via a series of shafts and joints, which transmitted suitable power when flailing. There were 43

Breach marking light dispenser for the Crab (Tank Museum).

heavy chains attached to the drum, together with a wire cutter at either end. On reaching a minefield the rotor was started and the Crab beat its way slowly forward at about 2½ mph. It cleared a lane some nine feet wide, hopefully detonating all the mines in its path. Naturally they did not always explode every mine, as those in sheltered hollows, for example, might escape, but in general terms they were most effective. The Crab could not, however, be used as a device to search for mines as flailing was such a slow and time consuming process, and the flail equipment had only a limited life.

THE MINE ROLLERS

Another way of setting off enemy mines was by the pressure exerted by some form of roller. As the roller would then be subject to the full blast of the mine, it had to be large enough and strong enough to withstand the explosion, or pivoted in such a way as to cause it to be swung clear out of harm's way by the initial blast. This was the theory behind the Canadian Indestructible Roller Device (CIRD), each roller being mounted on a swinging arm and covering the path in front of one tank track. After the explosion the roller was returned to its original position until the next contact.

Station-keeping equipment mounted on the rear of the Crab (Tank Museum).

Although the CIRD was trialled successfully, it was never used in action. While the British favoured the mine flail, the Americans undoubtedly preferred the mine roller, devoting a great deal of time and effort to experimenting with numerous different types. Perhaps the most successful and widely used went by the

This strange contraption was known as an anti-mine reconnaissance castor roller (AMRCR). The rollers were mounted on a frame which was fixed to the front of the tank and exploded mines by pressure (Tank Museum).

The T1E3 mine exploder was perhaps the best of the bunch and some 75 were built. Nicknamed 'Aunt Jemima', it saw operational service in Europe and Italy.

The mine exploder T9E1, which was first tested in April 1944, had a roller of lighter construction than its predecessor (the T9) but still cleared a ten-foot wide path.

nickname of 'Aunt Jemima'. All consisted basically of a number of large heavy, metal discs, grouped together into wheels. Sometimes the discs had toothed or serrated edges, others were smooth. Invariably they were extremely heavy and cumbersome. First trials of these mine exploders were carried out using tank recovery vehicles, the TRV's crane being essential to help manoeuvre the enormous wheels. However, this had the major disadvantage of no main armament, so later models were trialled with a gun tank, but poor mobility was always a drawback to their use, the heavy rollers easily becoming bogged in soft going.

EXPLOSIVE DEVICES

Yet another method was to set off some form of explosive device in order to detonate the mine. These ranged from adaptations of the Bangalore torpedo used in World War One to cut through barbed wire entanglements to pipes or hoses filled with explosive which were pushed or towed into a minefield and exploded. A typical example, the Snake, comprised a series of 20 foot lengths of three-inch diameter water piping, filled with explosive, when exploded it cleared a path about 20 feet wide. A Sherman was capable of pushing some 200 feet of Snake into a minefield or towing about 700 feet. A similar, but not so effective device, 'Tapeworm' comprised a towed canvas explosive-filled hose some 500 yards in length, while 'Conger' employed an aerial rocket to carry its hose across the minefield. This last method, although then in its infancy, is similar to the current in service British Giant Viper mine clearing device. Finally, there were various types of explosive rockets either trailer-borne behind the tank or carried on spigots mounted on a platform which took the place of the tank turret. The rockets were fired in a pattern, so as to explode the mines.

MISCELLANEOUS ANTI-MINE DEVICES

The photographs show the range of inventiveness which went into the problems of mine clearance. These included detection devices such as 'Lulu', a mine-resistant vehicle, the T15, and a series of mine ploughs which ploughed up the enemy mines and deposited them, hopefully, without setting them off, at the sides of the cleared furrow.

The T8 mine exploder had the nickname 'Johnnie Walker'. Plunger-type shock absorber exploder units were mounted in front of the tank and moved in a vertical direction by a powered gear drive from the sprockets. When the exploder tip detonated a mine the force of the blast was absorbed by the spring inside the unit plus oil under pressure. Initially there were to be 18 of the plunger units, but the trial model has only six. It was quite effective but difficult to manoeuvre over rough terrain.

The mine resistant vehicle T15 was built as an indestructible tank, based upon the Sherman, with thick belly armour, heavier suspension and tracks, and weighed 72,700 lb in total. It was followed by an even heavier version, the T15E1, and a T15E3 (based on the Pershing tank) was also proposed. It worked quite well, but the end of the war prevented completion of the project.

FLAILS IN ACTION

To discover how valuable were the Crab flails in action one needs only to look at the operations of 79th Armoured Division on D-Day, when mine clearing tanks formed a vital part of each of the assault teams in support of the leading troops. A flail regiment was organised in the same way as a normal armoured regiment, with an RHQ and three fighting squadrons. The squadron was the smallest sub-unit to be allocated to a formation for breaching purposes. It was organised into three troops of five tanks each. Three tanks working in echelon would make the initial breach (minimum 24 feet wide), with the other two remaining in reserve and at the same time available to give supporting fire, using their 75 mm guns as the other tanks would not fire while flailing. On normal ground flailing was only effective down to about five inches, so deep-laid mines would

German Crab flailing. The 43 chains that were attached to the rotor can be seen in action. At each end of the rotor is a cutter to deal with barbed wire.

This improvised flail tank was constructed for the USMC by the Seabees in November 1944.

113

be missed and might detonate long after many vehicles had crossed in safety. For D-Day, special assault teams were made up from the various component parts of 79th Armoured Division, the teams containing a mix of Crabs, AVREs and armoured bulldozers. Looking, for example, at the small portion of the invasion beaches, namely around Le Hamel and La Riviere, where units of 50th Northumbrian Division made the assault, six teams were allocated to each beach. At Le Hamel the teams had mixed fortunes. No 1 Team's landing craft was put out of action by enemy fire so could not land until the tide went out. No 2 Team landed and successfully cleared its lane, but in the process all three Crabs were knocked out, one being blown up on a mine which the chains had failed to set off, the other two being knocked out by enemy fire. This was the only successfully completed lane in that particular area and was used by all the DD tanks, SP guns and other armour landing on that beach during the first few days of the assault, so its role was critical. The other three teams at Le Hamel fared better, all completing their lanes despite most of the Crabs becoming casualties.

Following the fortunes of the leading Crab of No 1 Team at La Riviere beach one gets a more detailed account of the action: 'The leading Crab of No 1 Team (Lieutenant B. Pear, Westminster Dragoons) flogged its way up the shore between the obstacles, reached the road which ran directly behind the beach, turned North and followed the turning which led to "Lavatory Pan villa". He went over the ditch-crossing which had not been blown, passed the house and found a large crater. The squadron commander was informed and an AVRE successfully laid its SBG bridge. The task of clearing a route to Vers-sur-Mer was thus completed. Lieutenant Pear then skirted the villa to the west and flailed as far as the next crossing parallel to the abandoned road, meeting no mines. Major Sutton joined him and a lane of two tanks' width was thus cleared to give the DD tanks of C Squadron 4th/7th Dragoon Guards free access to the open country beyond.'[27] On the divisional front a total of seven lanes were successfully completed out of the 12 attempted, providing four safe exits on one brigade front and three on the other, through which the assaulting infantry and armour, and later a multitude of follow-up units moved safely on to the fields of Normandy.

SELF-PROPELLED ARTILLERY

In March 1942, the British Tank Mission and the US Tank Committee held a series of conferences in order to work out detailed plans for the co-ordination of American, British and Canadian war production. One of the major results of these meetings was to recommend a more balanced programme, increasing the production of armoured cars and self-propelled (SP) artillery at the expense of tanks. The startling success gained by German assault artillery was cited as evidence by the British, who urged the need for SP artillery on a massive scale. At that time the current American programme was only for the manufacture of just over 2,500 obsolescent 37 mm calibre guns, whereas the British-American conference recommended the production of over 15,000 SP weapons, ranging from 40 mm to 105 mm. These weapons were eventually known by a variety of nomenclatures – self-propelled mounts, gun motor carriages and howitzer motor carriages, and they served in many different roles, chiefly as anti-tank, anti-aircraft and mobile field artillery. In broad terms this proposed production programme was all put into effect at the expense of tank production; for example, while the number of medium tanks to be built was cut, SP weapons, built on the medium tank chassis, were added in their place. The end products were thus sufficiently similar for the shift to be described as 'a virtual renaming of part of our product'.[28]

Mention has already been made of some of the SP mounts based upon the M2 and M3 medium tanks; those using the M4 were in the main merely improvements of established weapon systems as guns to be carried became

T32, the first pilot 105 mm howitzer motor carriage, seen on tests at Fort Knox in February 1942.

heavier and calibres larger. For example, the highly effective 105 mm Howitzer Motor Carriage M7, of which some 3,500 were built between April 1942 and the end of the war, started life based upon the chassis of the medium tank M3, when two pilot vehicles were built in late 1941 and designated as the 105 mm HMC T32. After thorough testing and various modifications, the SP howitzer was standardised as the M7 in April 1942. The early production vehicles, like the prototypes, used the final drive housing and three-piece differential of the M3, while later production used both the three piece housing and the single piece casting of the M4. Similarly, the early models had the riveted lower hull and early vertical volute suspension, later replaced by the M4 welded type of hull and heavy-duty suspension bogies. At the same time as the M7 late model was being produced, Pressed Steel built a version based upon the M4A3, which was called the M7B1. 826 of this Ford-engined version were produced. The British called the M7 the Priest.

In the same way trials of an SP 155 mm gun were started in June 1941, using the M3 medium tank chassis. Known initially as the 155 mm GMC T6, the SP was standardised in 1942 as the 155 mm Gun Motor Carriage M12, and 100 were produced, being used to great effect in North-West Europe. As a result of this success the Artillery asked for more M12s, but there were no more of the original M1918 type of 155 mm gun left and trials proved that the M12 chassis just would not stand up to the mounting of a more powerful gun. Consequently, the successor to the M12, the 155 mm GMC M40, used late model Sherman components, including the HVSS and 23-inch tracks. Trials of the pilot models (known as the T83) were successful and over 400 of the new GMC were produced between February and September 1945, the SP being standardised as the M40 in May 1945. During the latter half of 1945, some two dozen M40s were converted to 8-inch Howitzer Motor Carriages T89. The majority of the M40 production came too late for use in World War Two, although two pilot vehicles were included in the ZEBRA Mission in February 1945 along with the new Pershing tank. The aim of this mission was to evaluate newly developed weapons under combat con-

Successor to the M12 was the 155 mm GMC T83, later standardised as the M40 in May 1945. It continued in service after the end of World War Two and was used to good effect in Korea. Some 24 M40s were converted to 8-inch HMC T89s.

The T52 multiple gun motor carriage was trialled in 1942 and comprised an M4 chassis with a ball-type turret on top, containing a 40 mm gun (seen here) with a .50-calibre HMG on each side (not mounted in this photograph). The gunner was located on the right of the 40 mm and had to reload the right-hand machine-gun as well as aiming and firing all three weapons. The loader on the left side was expected to do everything else, but just could not cope. The project ground on but was finally cancelled in October 1944.

ditions, the SP guns being used during the attack on Cologne. Other SP artillery to be trialled, using Sherman components, included a heavy 10-inch mortar and a 155 mm mortar which was to be mounted in a normal Sherman tank turret in place of the 75 mm. Interest in heavy SP mortars waned and both projects were cancelled without reaching production status.

ANTI-AIRCRAFT ARTILLERY

Another part of the Blitzkrieg which developed rapidly in the early war years was the employment of ground-attack aircraft. Anti-aircraft defence was therefore essential and if it was to be able to provide support for a mobile, armoured force, then it needed to be mounted upon a suitable tracked chassis. The British Crusader AA tank is a successful early example which was developed and brought into service in 1942 in various versions, mounting first a 40 mm Bofors and then twin 20 mm Oerlikon cannons. The Armored Force clearly had the same requirements and so various anti-aircraft guns mounted on the chassis of the medium tank were trialled. These ranged from single 40 mm guns, to twin and quad machine-guns, combination mounts and even to the mounting of a 90 mm AA gun – no doubt inspired by the success of the dreaded German 88 mm AA gun in the anti-tank role. None of these ever reached production status although, as the photographs show, they were built. The only AA weapon which actually reached the combat zone was a version of the Canadian Ram, called

90 mm gun motor carriage T53 after the fitting of a semi-circular shield to provide crew protection. It was found to be too unstable to be effective against high-flying aircraft, so was evaluated as a tank destroyer (hence the need for the shield) but was equally unsatisfactory in that role and was abandoned

Based upon the Canadian Ram tank, the Skink AA tank was the only successful AA tank to reach operational service. It mounted four quad 20 mm Polsten cannons.

the 'Skink', which mounted quad 20 mm Polsten cannons. During early 1945 a Skink was shipped over to Europe and used operationally by 1st Canadian Army. It was considered superior to the Crusader; however, by then there were few worthwhile aerial targets and although it proved quite effective against enemy ground forces, the project was quickly cancelled. It is interesting to see that, with the wide variety of air attack weapons, including helicopters, missiles and aircraft, AA tanks are nowadays making a comeback.

TANK DESTROYERS

The need to find a way to counter the highly successful German Blitzkrieg tactics in Poland and France, led the Americans to look urgently for an effective way of stopping tanks. The ease with which the German armour had sliced its way through French and British opposition in the heady days of 1940 had undoubtedly badly affected American morale, so it was essential to find new weapons that would disprove the invulnerability of the tank. At the time it was not considered that the best weapon to use against a tank was another tank. Instead, the War Department decided that the employment of large numbers of fast-moving, high-velocity anti-tank guns was the right answer and this led directly to the setting up of a separate Tank Destroyer Command.

The name 'Tank Destroyer' (TD) was deliberately chosen as it emphasised the aggressive role of the new force. Initially TD units were equipped with towed guns, but rapidly the tracked TD took over as the primary weapon. At its peak the TD Force numbered 106 active battalions, only 13 less than the total of conventional tank battalions. 'Seek, Strike and Destroy' was the motto of the Tank Destroyer Command and they rapidly proved themselves to be courageous and capable fighters. Despite an excellent war record the TD force was axed at the end of the war, because battle experience had shown that the more vulnerable TD, with its light armour and open turret, was not as versatile or cost-effective as the better-protected tank.

There were three main tracked tank destroyers, two of which were based largely upon the medium tank. The M10 Wolverine was the first to be built and began life in late 1941, when a 3-inch gun was mounted on a standard M3 chassis from which both the turret and side 75 mm gun sponson had been removed. It was known as T24, but trials soon showed that the design was too high and too complicated for mass production, so the project was cancelled in March 1942. It was quickly followed by the T40, which mounted a 3-inch AA gun in a low angle mounting, again on an M3 chassis. It lacked both speed and mobility but was considered adequate and 50 were ordered. Standardised as the GMC M9, only 28 of the necessary 3-inch guns could be obtained, so the project foundered and was cancelled in August 1942. Fortunately another project which had begun in April 1942 was proving more successful. Called the T35, it comprised a 3-inch gun mounted on the chassis of a Sherman M4A2. Later the T35 was replaced by an improved model, the T35E1, which had a lower silhouette, an angled hull (to deflect enemy shot), thinner armour to make it lighter and thus improve its mobility and a five-sided, open-topped, welded turret. Standardised in June 1942, it was designated as the GMC M10. Such was the demand for TDs that another Sherman chassis had to be used as well, the M4A3, resulting in the GMC M10A1. In all 4,993 M10s and 1,713 M10A1s were built, 1,648 of them being supplied to the British Army, who from late 1944 began converting them by replacing the 3-inch gun with their own more powerful 17-pdr. The result was a TD known as Achilles, the Mk IC being the M10 conversion and the Mk IIC from the M10A1. Basic specifications of the M10 are shown in the table on this page.

The next TD to be produced was the M18 Hellcat, but this was designed from scratch, although it did use some of the basic components of the medium tank – such as the engine and main armament (75 mm gun). It was a highly effective, fast TD, although much more lightly armoured than either the M10 or the last of the trio, the M36. The latter was the

M10 SPECIFICATIONS	
Crew	5 (commander, driver, and three gun crew)
Combat weight	65,200 lb
Length (gun forward)	22 ft 5 in (23 ft 10 in for Achilles with 17-pdr)
Width	10 ft
Height	9 ft 6 in (over AA machine-gun)
Armament :	
main	One 3-in Gun M7 (one 17-pdr Mk V on Achilles)
secondary	One .30-cal AA Browning machine-gun (also 2-in mortar on Achilles)
Armour thickness max/min	2.25 in/0.5 in
Engine	Twin GMC 6-71 diesels (M10); Ford GAA V-8 petrol (M10A1)
Max speed	30 mph
Radius of action	Approx 200 miles
Trench	7 ft 6 in
Vertical wall	2 ft
Fording depth	3 ft

most powerfully-armed of the three, its 90 mm M3 gun being more than a match for most enemy armour. Tests had begun in early 1943 to see if it was feasible to mount a 90 mm AA gun on to an M10 in place of the 3-inch gun. Test firings were successful, but it was evident that a completely new turret would have to be designed. Two pilot vehicles, based upon the M10A1, were completed, tested, proved satisfactory and designated as the GMC T71. 500 were ordered, but only 300 M10A1 chassis were available (ie, the basic chassis was, of course, that of the M4A3 medium tank), so the

The T35E1 was the improved model of the T35, with a lower silhouette and sloped armour on both hull an turret designed to deflect enemy fire. It was to be standardised in June 1942 as the GMC M10.

numbers were made up by converting M10A1s which had been returned from combat. Standardised as the GMC M36 in July 1944, there soon proved to be a great demand for the new, hard-hitting TD, so various other chassis had to be used, eg, standard hulls of M4A3 medium tanks (known as M36B1) and M10 hulls (known as M36B2). A total 2,324 of all three models was produced during the war.

There is no doubt that the TDs did a fine job and their crews were proud of the fighting capability of their lightly armoured vehicles. Here is how Paul Stevenson, late of C Company, 644th Tank Destroyer Battalion, re-

members those days: 'Our 3-inch (World War One US Naval AA) rifle was the best anti-tank weapon the US had, until near war's end, when they brought on the M36. Except for our twin 375 hp GMC Diesel engines (Marine), our chassis was the M4 tank chassis. But the added weight of our long, flat trajectory, high-velocity 3-inch (or 76.2 mm) gun forced two other weight add-ons: a 3,000 lb counter-balance at the turret's rear, and a heavy armored mantle at the front of the turret. All of this added some ten tons to a power train engineered to carry a total weight of only 31 tons. To offset this, they simply pared down the armor plate, all around. Our frontal glacis plate was $1\frac{1}{2}$ inches (the M4 was some six inches). Our side armor was $\frac{5}{8}$-inch thick ... I think the M4 was two inches or more.[29] Had this weight not been taken off, only Tarzan could have traversed the manual turret and fired the gun at anything, so this trade-off to get a good weapon was essential. It also meant that any 75 mm or 88 mm, and some smaller-bore AT weapons could kill us. Our side armor would not stop 20 mm (.50-caliber), either.

'The gun, the sighting, the solenoid firing device, the engines and power train (if one engine were hit, we could clutch it out, and get by (for a while) on one engine only) were all superb. December '44 introduction of the HVAP ammo (shaped charge) made our 3-inch guns even more effective. Even so, at much more than 200 yards' range, even our 3-inch APC ammo would not penetrate the Mark V's frontal glacis armor. Those we bested under fire were hit in the sides, the belly, or the rear. And we also knocked off tracks, leaving Jerry still able to fire his 75 mm at us, or other enemies of the Third Reich. Like most every-thing in war, the M10 was a trade-off.

'As for crew living, I'd much prefer 300 nights in Claridges than 300 nights in an M10. But the diesel power (other outfits had gasoline-powered, V8 Ford and Chrysler en-gines) left our fighting compartment and all interiors free of volatile fumes, so we did smoke, burned Coleman stoves (the coffee pot), warmed our "C" and ten-in-one rations, without risk.

'I myself lost two M10s and 80% of both crews to "fire", but in one case (Dinard and St Malo, France) one round of 75 mm hit the six rounds of 3-inch ammo in the turret "ready rack", and all six exploded as one, killing all the crew except the driver, who went out through the escape hatch in the floor, between his feet. And he spent years in the Army hospital burn wards, for skin grafts, etc ... and then died at 40 years, some 20 years after the war. In another, near Siegen, after the breakout of the Remagen Bridgehead, a Kraut put a round right through the star on the right side of the hull. We carried 54 rounds of 3-inch ammo in the sponsons at that level, and that went up in flames and explosions. All of that crew were burned to death, except the driver ... except this one forgot the floor hatch, and passed through the wall of fire then raging in the fighting compartment, to his rear. He also went through long months of burn treatments (face and hands), but is okay today.'

Paul goes on to describe a typical TD action which took place during the Battle of the Bulge: 'At 07:30 hrs, having just arrived at positions south-east of Wirtzfeld to cover possible German armor coming north from Bullingen and any threat to either Krinkelt or Wirtzfeld, Owen McDermott saw a column of an estimated 10 or 12 German tanks moving across his front at a range of 400-500 yds. He had two M10s take them under fire, knocking out two Mark IVs, the lead tanks. The rest of this column turned back, and disappeared in the fog, the woods, and were believed to be headed back to Bullingen. Suddenly, another column, with two Mark Vs in the lead, came up

the same road, at speed, bypassing their disabled comrades. Letting these get north to a distance of 750 yards, and get clear shots at their thinner sides, McDermott ordered his crews to fire at them. In moments, and after a very few shots, both Mark Vs were burning, and their crews jumping out and running around wildly. At this point, Owen (standing on the rear deck of his lead M10) grabbed the .50-caliber machine-gun, and started spraying the enemy crewmen and their infantry on the ground. Just then, a halftrack arrived in Mac's sights, to start collecting Germans, so he ordered a couple of rounds of 3-inch fired at the halftrack, sending it up in flames. At about 09:30 hrs, all other German tanks in that column had turned back, toward Bullingen, to rejoin (obviously now the Kampfgruppe Peiper column) and headed due west. These were the first, and last threats to either Wirtzfeld or Krinkelt from the south, but as you know, Peiper's column penetrated some 50-60 miles, well past Bastogne, into US lines and Rocherath-Krinkelt became the northern "shoulder" of the "Battle of the Bulge".

'An hour later, McDermott was relieved by two platoons (eight M10s) of Co A 644th, and sent north into perimeter positions in Rocherath, in support of defending 38th Infantry troops. His platoon got no Kraut tanks on the 18th (Day Two), but it was fitting that his

Overhead view of the GMC M36 turret with its 90 mm gun, mounted on the chassis of the M1 Hellcat.

gunners KOd two more tanks, and one SP in the final hours of Day Three, as the 38th and all supporting units were finally withdrawn to prepared defensive positions on a "better" shoulder along Elsenborn Ridge. In this battle, Owen lost Sergeant Tom Myers (WIA) and Sergeant Emory Ellis (WIA) only. One M10 was then commanded by its Corporal (later Sergeant) Gunner. The other was taken over by its T/5 Driver, later Sergeant Bill Hooper.'

TANK RECOVERY VEHICLES

Mention has already been made of the tank recovery vehicles M31 and M31B1 which were converted in some quantity from M3 and M3A3 medium tanks, over 800 being produced before the number of available M3s became too limited and the production of recovery vehicle based upon the Sherman was authorised. This happened in April 1943, when development of the T5, T5E1, T5E2, T5E3 and T5E4 was approved from the M4, M4A1, M4A2, M4A3 and M4A4 respectively. These TRVs were designed to have a fixed turret and an 'A' frame crane. The T7 was also

approved. This had a similar turret-mounted boom to the M31 and was based on the M4. The T5 series were found to be the best and were standardised as the M32, M32B1, M32B2, M32B3 and M32B4 respectively. They were all similarly equipped with a 60,000 lb winch driven off the propshaft which was mounted on beams behind the driver's seat with a centrally placed cable drum. As the photos show, the crane boom was hinged at the front of the hull and could be lowered over the rear decks for travelling, or towing.

The first conversions made were five M32B2s produced at the Lima Locomotive works in June 1943, over 1,500 of all types being produced by the end of the war, the majority being M32B1s. In addition, some 80 T14s were produced, which had wider tracks and a new boom lifting device. For protection the TRVs carried a .50 HMG on the turret ring, a .30 MG in the bow and on all models except for the T14, an 81 mm mortar was mounted on the front hull with 30 rounds of smoke ammunition carried. Towards the end of the war, the vehicles were fitted with HVSS, becoming the M32A1, M32A1B1, M32A1B2, and M32A1B3. They continued to give ster-

An M32 preparing to lift a Stuart light tank on to a transporter.

British version of the tank recovery vehicle was known as the Sherman ARV. Note that the complete turret has been removed and a jib crane fitted which had a lift capability of 6,720 lb. It was subsequently renamed as the Sherman ARVI when another version (the Sherman ARVII) was introduced which had a welded fixed structure in place of the tank turret. US versions were known as the Sherman ARVIII (Tank Museum).

ling service long after the end of hostilities. A number of M32A1B1s were converted into prime movers in early 1944 as there was a shortage of M6 high-speed tractors to tow heavy artillery pieces.

The British also developed tank recovery vehicles (called Armoured Recovery Vehicles (ARV) in British parlance), which were based upon the Sherman. The Sherman ARVI was a conversion from the standard tank, with the turret completely removed and large rectangular double doors replacing it in the hull roof. Twin .303 Bren MGs could be mounted on top in the hatch opening, and the bow-mounted MG was also retained. A 6,720 lb capacity jib crane was mounted on the front of the tank, equipped with a chain block and cable to lift engines and power trains, etc. On the rear was a swivelling connector to which could be attached Hollebone drawbars for towing AFVs (short bar for US vehicles, longer bar to reach the towing eyes on British AFVs). A later model, designated the Sherman ARVII, had its turret replaced by a welded, fixed structure which had a dummy gun barrel fixed to its front. It was equipped with a jib crane, 'A' frame and spade assembly on the rear of the hull, plus a winch run off the main engine. Sherman ARVIII was the designation given to any of the US M32 series of TRVs. Finally, for D-Day, a number of ARVIs were converted in to Beach Armoured Recovery Vehicles (BARV) by the addition of a tall, waterproofed superstructure.

THE AFTERMATH

Victory in Europe over the Germans in May 1945 saw the Sherman medium tank as the mainstay of the American Army, while many thousands were also serving with other Allied armies all over the world. At the Victory Parade celebrations held in Berlin in June 1945, 2nd Armored Division from General George Patton's famous Third Army took part with a mixture of modern and not so modern Shermans, as the photograph shows. Fighting, of course, continued in the Far East until the dropping of atomic bombs on Hiroshima and Nagasaki brought Japanese surrender and total victory in August 1945. From that moment on, the rôle and structure of the US Army overseas altered drastically. No longer was it a field army conducting combat operations, instead it became an Army of Occupation, like the armies of the other major victorious powers, based in static camps within the countries of its erstwhile opponents. The Sherman remained the standard medium tank both at home and abroad.

Shermans on parade. Tanks of 2nd Armored Division line up for inspection by the Secretary of War, Henr L. Stimson, accompanied by General George Patton 20 July 1945, in Berlin.

South Korea in the summer of 1950. At the start of the Korean War the state of armour in the US Army was a sad reflection on its considerable strength at the close of World War Two. A survey showed that only 900 M24 light tanks were serviceable out of a total of nearly 3,500, and that only 319 of the new M46 Patton tanks were as yet in service. The figures for mediums were a little better, there being 1,826 serviceable and 1,376 unserviceable.

OBSOLESCENCE

As far as the US Army was concerned, officially the Sherman became obsolete on 14 February 1957 with the issue of OTCM 36468, which reclassified to 'Obsolete Type' eight, various AFVs, including the 'Tank, Combat, Full-Tracked: Medium, 76 mm Gun, M4A3 (HVSS)'. The proceedings of the Subcommittee on Automotive Equipment were submitted to the Ordnance Technical Committee on that date and list the reasons why they included the M4A3 (HVSS): 'This item is added to the list by direction of DCS LOG, based on recommendation of the Material Requirements Review Panel, which considered the item unsuitable for current Army requirements.' They go on to explain that it has been replaced by: 'Tank, Combat, Full-Tracked: 90 mm Gun, M48 Series.'

The full recommendations of the Subcommittee were:

'a. That subject vehicles, together with guns, mounts, fire control and ammunition items peculiar thereto be reclassified to Obsolete Type (A complete list of the related items made obsolete by this action will be recorded at a later date by Read for Record action).

b. That all assets of subject vehicles be disposed of by salvage or other authorized means with the exception as stated in regard to the M46, M46A1 tanks.

c. That this action and material, components & related documents be UNCLASSIFIED.'[30]

The fifteen-member subcommittee was chaired by Lt Col M. A. Kinley of the Ordnance Corps, whose signature appears at the end of the recommendation. It was approved by the Ordnance Technical Committee on 14 March 1957 and later by the Secretary of the Army.

One of the postwar developments was the excellent M74 TRV, based upon the M4A3E8 chassis. This tank recovery vehicle had a dozer blade on the front, both for dozing and to stabilise the vehicle when the 'A' frame was in position. It had an internally-mounted winch with a 90,015 lb capacity. Armament was a single pintle-mounted .50 Browning HMG.

In addition to the thousands of Shermans still in service or being put into 'mothballs' in numerous strategically placed Ordnance vehicle parks in various parts of the world, the now quiet battlefields were littered with them. It was a marvellous time for the scrap metal dealers and I vividly remember while visiting an area of the Ardennes in the summer of 1948, watching scrap collectors at work, cutting up large numbers of tanks – including what appeared to be an almost complete regiment of Shermans which had been wiped out by a single well-sited Jagdtiger. Serviceable equipment was collected and taken to scrapyards, like the huge one at Sainte Anne near Antwerp. They were used to rebuild the armies of friendly, liberated countries, such as France and Belgium, and even those of erstwhile enemies like Italy. In the Pacific theatre the situation was very similar and here Operation ROLL-UP was put into action, which had the aim of collecting serviceable equipment and shipping it to Japan, where it was repaired under the auspices of the American Army of Occupation.

World events were to prove this a most fortuitous act, as it was only five years after the end of hostilities that the world was once again plunged into a major war, with the invasion of

Complete with bulldozer blade and deep fording equipment, this M4A43E8 (105 mm howitzer) belonging to the USMC is photographed during exercises at Mellieha Bay, Malta, August 194 (Author's collection (USMC)).

EUROPEAN ARMIES

The majority of re-emerging European armies relied heavily upon American equipment. For example, the very first tanks which the Belgian armoured corps acquired after the war were some second-hand Shermans which they purchased from the Sainte Anne scrapyard at scrap metal price! Their artillery already had a number of British 17-pdr anti-tank guns, so they tried mainly to buy Sherman Fireflies which mounted the same weapon. These tanks were given a thorough overhaul at the Racourt Arsenal and then issued to units, 2eme Lanciers receiving the first batch of 29 Sherman Hybrid ICs in 1949, the regiment having been re-formed the previous year. By June 1949, they had a total of 58 Sherman IC, plus six IB and three M32 TRVs. Next to receive the mediums were 1er Guides who acquired Sherman VCs in August 1950, followed by 3eme Lanciers in September 1950, who received Sherman IIAs direct from the US Army, and then 1er Lanciers in December 1950 with VCs. The 2eme Chasseurs à Cheval were given 17 Shermans for their tank squadron when they re-formed as a light cavalry battalion in May 1952. In total, the Belgians purchased over 200 Fireflies (plus 10 Stuart M5A1s and some M22 Locust light airborne tanks).

Additionally, 3eme Lanciers received some later model M4A1s mounting the 76 mm gun and fitted with HVSS, while a number of M4A3s with 105 mm howitzers were obtained to boost up the IBs (M4 with 105 mm) purchased in 1949, for the support platoons of every tank regiment. Also in 1950, the 21eme Bataillon d'Artillerie received some GMC M36 (90 mm) and 23eme Bataillon d'Artillerie some Achilles tank destroyers (17-pdr). From 1952 onwards, the Sherman gun tanks were replaced first by Pershings and then by Patton I and II from the United States. The Pattons were themselves replaced by 328 Leopard I, bought from West Germany in the late 1960s.

In addition to the gun tanks and tank destroyers, the Belgians had obtained a number of M32 and M32A1B1 TRVs, which served in cavalry units equipped with Sherman and later with most other armoured units. The 6eme Genie (engineers) had a number of Sherman dozers, one or two Crabs, one DD and even an Ark as well. Last of the Sherman derivatives in service with the Belgian armoured corps was the M74 TRV, which remained in use until it was replaced by the Bergepanzer Leopard.

The Free French forces had been almost exclusively equipped with American material,

A M32 Tank Recovery
Vehicle of the Austrian
Army, which remained
in service until they
were replaced by the
M88 ARV when M60A1
main battle tanks were
introduced (HBF
Heeresbild).

Sherman Firefly of
the Belgian Army on
parade. The Firefly was
the first postwar
medium tank to be
retained by the Belgians
for their armoured
forces (Belgian Army
Museum).

the Sherman being the main tank. Such Free French armour as Gen Leclerc's 2nd Armoured Division, which had fought as part of the US Third Army and was appropriately given the task of liberating Paris in August 1944, had Sherman tanks, M10 and M36 tank destroyers, TRVs, etc. An immediate postwar check would have shown many Shermans of all types in French service.

Colonel (retired) Herve Doyen remembers those days very well as he was just beginning his army service. He told me: 'As far as I remember the French Army ended World War Two with three armoured divisions, each with three regiments of Shermans (each approx 55 tanks). All types of M4 were represented from the very early models with prominent driver hatches, single turret hatch, narrow gun mantlet and small 75 mm gun turrets – mainly A1, A2, A4, cast or laminated hulls, to the last A3 type with a big turret, large gun mantlet and 75 mm or 76 mm gun, big oval driver hatches with periscopes instead of vision slits. Those tanks remained in active service up to 1949–51 when they were stored for reserve regiments. They were replaced by the M4A1E8 (76 mm gun) with a cast hull, given by the US under their 'Mutual Defense Assistance Program (MDAP)' and supplemented, as far as I remember, with some M4A4s with narrow tracks, refitted to A1 standard, which had been brought from US surplus. All Shermans disappeared from the French Army inventory when they were replaced in 1952–55 by M47 and were possibly returned to the US. To the best of my knowledge Shermans were not used by the French Army in Indochina or Algeria, but this needs checking as the information is now hidden deep in my old skull!'

An M4A1(76) of the
Belgian Armoured
Corps on exercise
(Belgian Army
Museum).

Sherman M4A3
mounting a 105 mm
howitzer coming off a
landing craft during
exercises in Belgium.
Such tanks were
obtained for the suppor
platoons of each
regiment (Belgian
Army Museum).

Two smartly-dressed
members of 23rd
Artillery Battalion pose
in front of their M10
tank destroyer (Belgian
Army Museum).

A Priest, 105 mm
howitzer M7, of the
Belgian artillery on
exercise (Belgian Army
Museum).

covering an M24 Chaffee from a ditch, is Belgian TRV really s to strain – note how e back end is right off e ground! (Belgian my Museum).

graphs showing Sherman M4A2 of the Regiment Blindé Colonial d'Extreme-Orient in action in December 1951, while M36B tank destroyers were deployed as late as July 1953 in the Tonkin area, as Col Doyen has said, to safeguard against a potential armoured threat from China in support of the Viet Minh.

As already stated, I do not believe Shermans were used in Algeria. Certainly, Jacques Soustelle, who was appointed Governor General there in 1955 had this to say about the use of tanks: 'To send in tank units, to destroy villages, to bombard certain zones, this is no longer the fine comb, it is using a sledge-hammer to kill fleas.' Later on, light armour was used to support the gendarmerie in Algiers, but not medium tanks. The most recent use of Sherman in this conflict occurred in France itself, when, during the state of emergency declared by General de Gaulle against the OAS, old Shermans were brought out to protect government buildings in Paris. A photograph of some Shermans outside the National Assembly, taken on 23 April 1961, appeared in Alistair Horne's book *Savage War of Peace, Algeria 1954–1962*, together with the following comment: 'Elderly Shermans of 2nd World War vintage rumbled out from retirement to take up positions outside the Assembly and other government buildings. Discouragingly some broke down and had to be towed across the Concorde.'

Of course, the French did not dispose of the Sherman when they started to build their own postwar tanks. They adapted various turrets and tank guns to lengthen the M4's useful life, obligingly selling them to *both* sides during the Arab/Israeli conflicts, which I have covered later in this chapter. These included mounting the FL 10 turret (75 mm gun) from the AMX 13 and the excellent 105 mm gun onto the basic M4A1 chassis to transform it into the 'Super Sherman'.

The Italians had become co-belligerents against the Germans as a result of the Armistice signed with the Allies in September 1943. Therefore, their forces were not disarmed at the end of the war, but restrictions were nevertheless placed upon the numbers, size and types of AFVs, weapons and equipment they were allowed to hold. Thus, in order to make up on numbers of tanks, the Italian armoured forces had to enlist the help of the scrap dealers who were operating the large dumps where the departing Allied troops had

Colonel Doyen also told me about other variants: 'In 1944, infantry and armoured divisions contained regiments of tank destroyers (each 36 M10s). They were partly replaced by a mixture of M26 and M36 in 1951–53, which in turn were abandoned when AMX 13 were put into mass production. M36 were used in North Vietnam (Tonkin) in 1951–54, I do not know to what extent, but probably not more than two or three squadrons. The turret roof protection was improved against vertical fire, grenades and infantry assault. One of the best ways of dealing with infantry assault was to fire the gun at maximum elevation and wait for the devastating effect of the noise generated by the muzzle brake!'

While I could find no evidence of Shermans being used in Algeria, they were certainly present in Indo-China, although of course light tanks predominated in the French Expeditionary Force that landed there in October 1945, to combat the ever-increasing insurgent forces of Ho Chi Minh. Lieutenant (now Major General, retired) Richard Jerram, late Royal Tank Regiment, visited Indo-China and wrote in a subsequent article published in *The Tank* magazine: 'The tanks in Indo-China are mostly Shermans and Chaffees with 75 mm guns, and M5s, some with 37 mm guns and some with 75 mm howitzers. Although out of date, the lighter tanks were well suited for the task, for the present day heavy American and British tanks would be quite useless over the narrow tracks and flimsy bridges of the country, and even more prone to become bogged in the swamps and paddy fields, than the ones in use.' Other sources confirm this, with photo-

parked their surplus weapons before going home. They were able to find plenty of tanks and other AFVs, artillery pieces, etc, although all had been demilitarised by having their weapons spiked by drilling holes through the gun barrels so that they could not be fired. The Italians got around this problem by manufacturing special sleeves that were shrunk onto the barrels, covering the holes, so that the weapons could be fired again – how safely one does not know!

Between 1945 and 1952, the Italian armoured corps had most types of Sherman gun tanks and Sherman derivatives in service and I am grateful to Colonel Tom Huggan, OBE, of the NATO Defence College in Rome and Maj Gen (Retd) Luigi Campagna, for providing the following figures:

Sherman gun tanks. Between 1,800 and 2,000 were held. No exact figure is available due to the illegal 'transfers' of AFVs from the dumps. Types included: M4, M4(105), M4A1, M4A1(76), M4A2, M4A2(76), M4A3, M4A3(76), M4A3(105) and M4A4. Most numerous were M4A2 and M4A2(76).

Sherman derivatives. M10 (numbers not known); M36 (259 held); M32 (40 held); M74 (numbers not known); M7 Howitzers (354 held); also some artillery OP tanks and M1 bulldozers.

KOREA

The initial phase of the Korean War, which began with the Communist invasion of South Korea on 25 June 1950, saw first the weak defending forces, and then those of the United States which had been hastily sent over from Japan to help stem the tide, having to give ground in front of the much more powerful, better-equipped and motivated forces of North Korea. The invaders were spearheaded by Russian-built tanks, which quickly swept aside the lightly-equipped South Koreans, who lacked any effective anti-tank weapons. The first American tanks to arrive in Korea were some M24 Chaffees, which mounted a 75 mm gun adapted from the heavy aircraft cannon as used in the B-259 Mitchell bomber. The Chaffee was the standard US light tank of the day and the best light tank of World War Two, but it was no match for the North Korean T34/85s which were even now pushing the United Nations' forces into a small perimeter around the port of Pusan. Thanks to Operation

ROLL-UP, as mentioned earlier, there were a large number of heavier, more powerful tanks in Japan, many of which had been given a complete rework at the Tokyo Ordnance Depot. These included various models of the Sherman. As soon as the war started work at the depot was increased dramatically, a staggering 8,000 wheeled and tracked vehicles being refitted during the months of July and August 1950. As well as repairing and renovating ex-World War Two equipment for use in Korea, the depot also instituted a crash programme of modifying certain vehicles and weapons to make them more effective. For example, M4A3 tanks had their 75 mm guns replaced by the much more effective 76 mm. The M7 Howitzer Motor Carriage was modified so that its 105 mm could reach a maximum elevation of 67° (normal maximum elevation was 35°) so it was able to fire over the steep Korean hills.

The first Shermans to reach Korea belonged to A Company of the 8072nd Medium Tank Battalion, a provisional organisation which had been activated in Japan. They reached Pusan on the last day of July, were moved forward by rail the following day and were in action less than 24 hours later. The rest of the battalion arrived on 4 August and three days later the unit was redesignated as the 89th Tank Battalion. More tanks were by then on their way from the USA; the SS *Luxembourg Victory*, for example, left San Francisco on 26 July carrying 80 medium tanks, and by the third week in August there were over 500 American mediums (Shermans, Pershings and M46 Pattons) within the Pusan perimeter, 20 of which had by then been knocked out by enemy action.

As the desperate position in the Pusan salient was slowly stabilised, thanks mainly to the tremendous sea and air support which was provided to back up the UN ground forces, the Eighth United States Army (as the ground troops were now collectively called), were able to go on to the offensive and to push the enemy back. They did not stop at the frontier, but went on into North Korea and all the way up to the Manchurian border. During these heady days there were numerous tank battles in which the Sherman was matched against the T34/85. Despite the heavier calibre of the enemy tank gun, the Sherman proved itself superior on many occasions, thanks to its better gun control equipment and stabiliser.

The war had swung completely in favour of the UN forces and the Supreme Commander, General Douglas MacArthur, was confidently predicting 'Home for Christmas'. Then the unthinkable happened, the Chinese entered the war in support of the North Koreans and launched a massive offensive with over 180,000 troops flooding over the border. Overwhelmed by sheer numbers, the US Eighth Army was driven back in considerable confusion and in bitter cold winter weather. General Walker, Eighth Army commander, managed to stabilise the situation on the 38th Parallel, but only for a short while, then the enemy pushed on, capturing the South Korean capital of Seoul in early January. General Walker was tragically killed in a Jeep accident and his place taken by General Matthew Bunker Ridgway – known somewhat irreverently by his troops as 'Old

Iron Tits' because of his penchant for wearing hand grenades in certain places! The Sherman did its bit during the retreat, but inevitably in the terrible conditions, many tanks were lost.

By mid-January it was clear that the enemy had run out of steam and Ridgway was able to go on to the offensive, retake Seoul and stabilise the front again roughly on the 38th Parallel. There followed then the static period of the war, with tanks being used as pillboxes rather than as mobile armoured fighting vehicles. Enemy armour all but disappeared from the battlefield and the tank was used mainly as an infantry support weapon, which included 'bunker-busting'. It was to be almost two years before the armistice was signed on 27 July 1953, after many months of desultory peace talks. All this time the static war continued, with both sides dug into opposing hilltops,

with tanks providing covering fire for the numerous infantry raids and patrols into the 'No Man's Land' that lay between the hills.

In addition to the US Army Shermans, the US Marine Corps was equipped with the medium tanks, as were the Canadians who had a tank squadron attached to the British armoured regiment of the Commonwealth Division. As a member of that armoured regiment, commanding a troop of Centurions on 'the Hook', I remember going to visit the Canadian tank positions, to admire their admirable M4A3E8(76)Ws, but thinking that I definitely preferred my better-protected Centurion. Undoubtedly, the Sherman tank did well in Korea, although its firepower fell well below that of the 90 mm of the Pershing and Patton, or the 20-pdr of the Centurion. Nevertheless, its reliability and manoeuvrability enabled Sherman crews to reach some quite unexpected places, as is evidenced by the following account of an action in March 1951, which was reported in *Combat Actions in Korea*, published by the Office of the Chief of Military History, United States Army, in 1954: 'Members of Company A 89th Medium Tank Battalion, crawled out of their sleeping bags at 03:30 on 7 March 1951. Breakfast was

scheduled at 03:45, the attack at 06:15. It was snowing, the heavy wet flakes, which melted soon after they fell, made the ground wet and slippery. Through the darkness and the usual early morning fog, the drivers went off to start the engines of their tanks so that they could warm up during breakfast.

'Bivouacked in the half-destroyed village of Kwirin-ni, Company A was ready to move as soon as the men finished breakfast and rolled up their sleeping bags. The company's 15 tanks and one tank recovery vehicle were dispersed among the buildings of the village, carefully located so that each would occupy its designated position in the column when it moved on to the road. The vehicles were already loaded with ammunition, carrying, in addition to the regular load of 71 rounds, 54 rounds that each crew had stacked on the rear deck of its tank. Fastened to the eight tanks that were to be at the head of the column were trailers, each carrying nested 12-man assault boats.

'Company A's mission for 7 March 1951 was to support the 25th Infantry [Division] in its assault crossing of the Han River. For the operation the tank company was attached to the infantry regiment, and further detailed to support the 3rd Battalion. Orders for the crossing, originating at Eighth Army, reached the 35th Infantry on 2 March. Regimental and battalion officers had begun at once to plan for the crossing and to train troops in the use of assault boats. Commanders, flying in liaison planes above the river, had searched for possible crossing sites. The Intelligence and Reconnaissance Platoon patrolled the south bank of the river to get specific information.

'Since the engineers had estimated that the Han River would be seven to nine feet deep at the time of the crossing, division and regimental orders included no plan to get tanks across the river during the assault phase. There was a plan, however, to construct a 50-ton-capacity floating bridge, which the engineers anticipated would be in use by early evening of the first day of the assault. After delivering fire across the river in support of the infantry crossing, the tanks were to continue direct fire support of the ground movement until they could cross on the bridge.

'As the planning progressed, Lieutenant Colonel Welborn G. Dolvin (commander of the 89th Tank Battalion) considered the possibility of getting tanks across the river in time to give close and effective support while the infantrymen were expanding their bridgehead. After reconnoitring the river bank and making several flights over the area, Colonel Dolvin suggested this possibility to the commander of Company A (Captain Herbert A. Brannon). He did not order Captain Brannon to attempt the crossing but only suggested that he fully investigate the possibilities, and that the advantages of giving tank support when the infantrymen most needed it warranted the risk involved. "It's worth a gamble," Dolvin said. Captain Brannon went to the engineers for more information about the depth of the water and the condition of the river bottom. Unfortunately, there was scant information on either, since the Chinese kept the river effectively covered with machine-gun fire both day and night. Captain Brannon studied aerial photographs of the crossing site and decided to gamble one tank on the crossing.

'On 4 March Brannon moved his tank company into a forward assembly area at Kwirin-ni about two miles from the proposed crossing site. That evening he called his platoon leaders to his mud hut and told them he intended to attempt to ford the river. His plan was to send one tank, towing a cable from the winch of the tank recovery vehicle, across the river. If the water proved to be too deep and the tank swamped out, the recovery vehicle on the south bank could pull it back. If the tank made it to the north bank, the others would follow the same route. The leader of the 3rd Platoon (Lieutenant Thomas J. Allie) volunteered to take the first tank into the water.

'The next morning Captain Brannon made a reconnaissance of the south bank of the Han. Hills and embankments on the right and in the central part of the regimental zone fell abruptly to the river. Only on the left, in the 3rd Battalion's sector, were the banks gentle enough to permit a crossing. This area, at the point where the Pukhan River joins the Han, was of necessity the crossing site for all assault units of the 35th Infantry. About a thousand yards upstream from the confluence of the rivers, there was a small, flat island dividing the Han into two channels, the near about 250 feet wide and the far about 200.

'Captain Brannon walked along the river bank until he was opposite the island or sand bar. Aerial photographs indicated he would find the most promising route at the west end of this island. After choosing a route for the tank crossing, he selected positions from which all three platoons could best support the crossing of the infantrymen.

'Since all movement to the river bank on 7 March would be hidden by darkness, tank-platoon leaders, accompanied by Captain Brannon, made their own reconnaissance on 6 March, locating the routes and the positions they would occupy.

'Engineers, responsible for furnishing and manning the assault boats, asked Captain Brannon to haul these craft to the river bank. There were two reasons for this: the engineers feared their trucks would get stuck in the loose sand near the river, and the regiment was anxious to have as few vehicles as possible on the roads leading to the crossing site on the morning of the assault. Each trailer carried five assault boats. Engineers were to ride on the trailers to the crossing site, unhook them, and then remain until the infantrymen arrived to put the boats into the water. After dropping the trailers, the tanks would proceed to their selected positions and prepare to fire. The schedule called for the tanks to fire a 20-minute preparation beginning at 05:55. At 06:15 infantrymen of the 3rd Battalion, 35th Infantry, would push the assault boats into the water and

row toward the hostile north bank of the river.

'Quietly, early on the morning of 7 March, Company A tankers finished breakfast, rolled up their sleeping bags, and then moved the tanks on to the road. When Captain Brannon ordered the column forward at 04:30, it had stopped snowing. The tanks moved slowly; the tank commanders did not want to make unnecessary noise by racing the engines, and it was too dark at the time for the drivers to see more than the outline of the road.

'Exactly as planned, the tank column proceeded to the river bank, stopped only long enough for the engineers to uncouple the trailers, then continued by platoons to firing positions. It was about 05:45. From across the river came the sound of occasional shell bursts. The preparation fire was not scheduled until 20 minutes before jump off. At 05:55 four battalions of 105 mm howitzers, a battalion of

155 mm howitzers and a regiment of British guns commenced firing on previously designated targets. Captain Brannon's tanks opened direct fire against targets on the north bank of the Han. For this fire, the crews used the ammunition loaded on the rear decks of the tanks, keeping the regular load of ammunition for use if they could successfully ford the river.

'It was still so dark that the tankers could see only the hazy outline of hills across the river. At 06:15, on schedule, infantrymen pushed assault boats into the water, and the assault wave, still partly hidden from the enemy by the dim half-light of early morning, started across the river. The infantrymen crossed several hundred yards below the sand bar, following a different route than that the tankers expected to take.

'The crossing progressed on schedule although enemy machine-gun fire punched

A mixed column of Shermans and Pershings supporting infantry of the USMC during their advance Hongchon, Korea, on March 1951 (Author's collection (USMC)).

small holes in several of the boats, wounding some of the occupants. Once across the river, the assault companies came under concentrated small-arms fire soon after leaving the gentle rise on the north river bank. At the same time, enemy artillery fire began falling on the south bank. Besides interfering with activities on that side of the river, the fire destroyed sections of a foot bridge then under construction.

'Lieutenant Colonel James H. Lee (infantry battalion commander) and Captain Brannon watched the river-crossing operation from the battalion's observation post. At 07:40, when he received word that all assault units of his battalion were across, Colonel Lee, who was skeptical of the success of the crossing, told Captain Brannon that the north bank was secure. "You can try crossing if you wish."

'Captain Brannon called Lieutenant Allie, who had offered to take the first tank into the water.

'Already within 200 yards of the river, the two vehicles moved to the edge of the water and stopped to connect the winch cable from the recovery vehicle to Lieutenant Allie's tank. About 08:00 Allie's tank went into the water, heading toward the west (downstream) end of the sandy island near the middle of the river. Lieutenant Allie stood erect in the open hatch, calling out instructions to the driver over the tank intercommunication system. The water was only about three feet deep, and since the Sherman tank was designed to ford water to that depth, there was no difficulty except that the speed of the tank, limited by the speed at which the motor-driven winch on the recovery vehicle could pay out the cable, was slow. After the tank had gone two-thirds of the distance to the island, the winch suddenly caught. The moving tank dragged the other vehicle for several feet, and then the cable broke, pulling apart at the coupling fastened to Lieutenant Allie's tank. Relieved to find the tank able to move freely, the tank driver (Sergeant Guillory Johnson) increased his speed. Within a few minutes after leaving the south bank, the tank reached the lower end of the sand bar.

'Originally, Lieutenant Allie had planned to proceed straight across, but once on the island, he could see at its east end what appeared to be footings for an old bridge. Crossing to the up-river end of the island, Lieutenant Allie turned into the water again. The tank dipped steeply into water that momentarily covered the hatches over Sergeant Johnson and his assistant driver, wetting both men. An experienced tank driver, Johnson at once increased the speed of the tank to keep the water from closing in behind the tank and drowning out the engine. The tank climbed out of the water at each of the three old earthen bridge footings but, after a few seconds, it would plunge again into the water deep enough to come up to the turret ring. Nevertheless, after being in the water for two minutes or less, the tank reached the opposite bank.

'After radioing back for the next tank in line to follow, Lieutenant Allie moved forward a short distance and then waited for the rest of his platoon. SFC Starling W. Harmon, following the same route with his tank, joined his platoon leader within five minutes. Wanting to have only one tank in the river at a time, Lieutenant Allie waited until Sergeant Harmon was on the north bank of the Han River before calling for the third tank. Because its escape hatch had jarred loose during the firing that morning, the third tank flooded out and stalled in the comparatively shallow water south of the island. Lieutenant Allie ordered his two remaining tanks, one at a time, to proceed around the stalled tank and cross.

'With two tanks, Lieutenant Allie set out at 08:30 to join the infantry. Having advanced a little more than a thousand yards, the infantrymen had stalled temporarily near a road that cut across the tip of land between the Pukhan and the Han. Enemy fire coming from a small hill and from a railroad embankment 600 yards ahead had stopped them. The two tanks moved forward, directing their fire against the small hill. When fire from the hill stopped, the two tank crews turned their cannon towards the railroad embankment. There were six freight cars standing on the tracks. They had been burned and shot up, apparently during an air raid. The Chinese had placed three machine-guns to fire under the cars into the area to the south. With their own machine-guns and 12 or 15 rounds from their cannon, the tank crews quickly silenced the enemy guns. The infantrymen moved up even with the two tanks, again 600 yards. As the infantrymen moved beyond the railroad tracks, following the two tanks which ranged ahead, three other enemy machine-guns commenced firing. Lieutenant Allie spotted one, laid on it with the 76 mm gun and fired two rounds, the second of which threw parts of bodies and weapons into the air.

The other two tanks of Lieutenant Allie's platoon arrived in time to take part in the firing, and a tank commanded by Master Sergeant Curtis D. Harrell located and silenced another machine-gun. Then, all four tanks raked the enemy positions with their coaxial machine-guns during a 30-minute period while the front line advanced approximately 700 yards to the objective.

'In the meantime, as soon as Lieutenant Allie's tanks were on the north bank, Captain Brannon started another platoon across. Within 20 minutes these five tanks were moving forward to support another infantry company and the last platoon of tanks began to cross. By 10:00 all Company A's tanks except one were moving forward with the assault companies; by noon Colonel Lee's 3rd Battalion had reached its objective. The remaining tank, which had flooded out earlier in the morning when its escape hatch fell out, was repaired by mid-afternoon and successfully crossed the river. The river crossing was a success and, as Colonel Lee believed, the close support furnished by the tanks was a big factor in the outcome of the operation.'

ISRAEL

Israel has undoubtedly made more use of the reliable old Sherman tank than any other nation in the world since the end of World War Two. When the tiny state of Israel was founded in May 1948, their armoured forces consisted of an odd assortment of makeshift, old, obsolescent AFVs, including four gun tanks – two Cromwells and two Shermans. The first of the Shermans was 'acquired' for the newly-emerging Israeli Defence Forces (IDF) by very devious means. It was at the time when, in the spring of 1948 during the last days of the Mandate, the British were hurriedly trying to get rid of the vast mass of AFVs, other vehicles, ammunition, arms and equipment, which had been steadily built up in the enormous rear base area around the port of Haifa. Large quantities of ammunition were sunk in the bay, while the AFVs were dragged up the Carmel road and then pushed off the top of a steep ridge, to fall to their destruction hundreds of feet below.

The Israeli arms acquisition group of Haganah in Haifa decided they would try to get hold of at least one of the tanks, as they well

A demonstration showing tank-infantry co-operation, features an M4A3E8 of 72nd Tank Battalion, 2nd Infantry Division, and men of the 32nd ROK Regiment, 2nd ROK Division, on 20 March 1952 (Author's collection (US Army))

knew they would be faced by a concerted Arab attack from all sides, once the British departed. Finding a sympathetic ear among the British troops whose job it was to carry out the destruction of the AFVs, the Jews were able to arrange for the clandestine abduction of one of the Shermans, while it was on its way up the mountain by night. It was transferred to a waiting Jewish transporter and spirited away to Tel Aviv, while the obliging British soldiers signed the necessary forms to confirm its destruction. Their prize, sadly, was in terrible order, its engine unserviceable, its suspension missing several bogies, numerous trackplates missing and, worst of all, lacking its guns and sighting equipment. It was necessary for the Haganah to go out and fight for the spare parts they needed from the already evacuated REME dumps in the Lydda area, where clashes with the Arabs were now daily occurrences. The need for trackplates was eventually solved when someone remembered the lengths of track laid by the British on the beach in Haifa Bay, near the base workshops, to facilitate vehicle movement in the soft sand. A 20 mm Hispano Suiza cannon was mounted

externally on top of the turret and the first IDF medium tank was ready for action!

The Sherman, an M4A2, had begun its military service when it had been supplied to the British in the Middle East in early 1943 and had initially served with the Royal Wiltshire Yeomanry. Now it was given the name *Tamar*, after a girlfriend of one of the crew. *Tamar* saw action almost immediately, defending Jewish settlements around Jenin, but it was soon clear that the external armament was most unsatisfactory as the crew members had to expose themselves completely when firing or reloading. Some old 75 mm guns had been obtained from arms dumps in Italy and one was fitted to the tank. At the same time, divers went down into Haifa Bay for the dumped ammunition which, after drying out, proved perfectly serviceable despite weeks under water. However, the tank was still without most of its optics, so accurate gunlaying was impossible.

A second Sherman, later called *Meir,* was also obtained from a British ordnance dump, reconditioned and fitted with a newly-arrived 75 mm gun. It was an M4A1 and was manned by an all-British crew when it went into action

These M1 Shermans (M4A1(76)W) are replenishing with fuel and ammo, near Jebel Libni during Operation Kadesh, 1956 (IDF Museum).

An early Israeli Sherman which has been re-armed with the German Krupp 1911 75 mm field gun, obtained from Switzerland (IDF Museum).

The M51 Sherman,
which was a modified
version of the M4A3E8,
designed to take the new
French 105 mm gun.
Note smoke dischargers
on sides of turret and
the excellent external
towage (IDF).

for the first time during the capture of Beer-sheba. Both Shermans then took part in operations in Sinai and were in the vanguard as the Israeli forces approached El Arish aerodrome. Unfortunately, *Tamar* broke down, shed a track and the crew, having no tools or spares, were unable to fix it. Following political pressure, the IDF had to withdraw in some haste from Sinai, and *Tamar* had to be destroyed in situ. It has remained there ever since throughout all the subsequent campaigns, a silent, rather forlorn reminder of those early desperate days.

By now a few more Shermans had arrived in Israel, having been purchased from as far afield as the Philippines. They formed part of 82nd Tank Battalion and saw action with *Meir* in the last battles of the War of Independence, which ended in the early hours of 7 January 1949. Following the armistice more and more Shermans were acquired from the arms dumps in Italy and elsewhere, including some M4A1s fitted with 105 mm howitzers which had been

demilitarised by the Americans by having holes drilled in their gun barrels. Initially the guns were put back into action merely by fitting close metal sleeves over the holes, but they still lacked any optical equipment which made accurate shooting quite impossible. Fortunately a better solution was on hand. The Israeli arms buyers were able to find some old World War One-vintage 75 mm Krupp M1911 field guns in Switzerland, where they had been stored for years, deep in Swiss ordnance depots in the mountains. Obsolete but unused, with a large amount of ammunition available, they were quickly purchased and adapted to fit on to the existing 105 mm howitzer loading mechanism. One can imagine how the ingenuity of the Israelis was taxed to the full finding ways of mounting the Krupp barrels with the minimum of specialised tools. However, they managed to achieve a workable solution and the new tanks were used to completely equip A Company of the 82nd. B Company was not quite so lucky, they had a mixture of old

M50 SP howitzers on parade. Note driver on left of the front-mounted engine. Designed in France to meet the requirements of the IDF, the M50 entered service in 1963 (Christopher Foss (IDF)).

Soltam L33 155 mm SP gun/howitzers on parade in Jerusalem in 1975. The L33 entered service in 1973 and was first used operationally during the October War (Christopher Foss (IDF)).

M4A2s, M4A3s and even a Firefly for which they had no ammunition! The Armour School at Ramle had three Shermans – all different Marks – and was very short of main gun ammunition, so that all training had to be carried out using co-axial machine-guns. In an article on those early days of the IDF, the Israeli magazine *Born in Battle* recounts the story of one of the few main armament live firing demonstrations, held at Ramle in 1951, designed to show the audience of senior officers the effectiveness of tanks in the close-support role. The tanks advanced, firing HE from their 'ill-fitting contraptions', some of the rounds exploding at random within 30 m of the startled audience. Thereafter, as the writer explained: '. . . there was a long and embarrassing lull'.

It was of course essential for the Israelis to find better tanks, particularly as their Arab foes were now receiving more sophisticated weaponry from the Soviet Bloc, including T34/85s and SU152 SPs. Fortunately help was at hand, in that the French, realising that Nasser was actively supporting the Algerian terrorists, decided that they would allow the Israelis to purchase more modern weapons. These included AMX13 light tanks and surplus M4A1 Shermans, which had been modernised by the fitting of the 76 mm gun. They began arriving in 1956 some time before the start of the Sinai campaign. About the same time the French were engaged in other development which would further prolong the battle record of the Sherman. They had for some time been working on a very good new 75 mm tank gun, based upon the long-barrelled German 7.5 cm Kwk 42 (L/70), which had been the main armament of the Panther. The new gun had a muzzle velocity of more than 1,000 m/sec as compared with the 600 m/sec of the Sherman M3 gun.

The French had, of course, already mounted the gun in an oscillating turret on the AMX13 light tank, but the IDF had serious doubts about the battleworthiness of the little 14½-ton tank when ranged against the Soviet giants. The Israelis had plenty of Sherman tanks, battleworthy and well liked by their crews, but undergunned, so the obvious answer was to try to mount the French gun (CN 75-50) on to the Sherman. A technical mission of Israeli tank experts was set up at Bourges Arsenal in France during 1954 and after numerous trials a final model was produced the following year. It had a special adaptation of the AMX 13

sighting gear and a modified ammunition feed. Later in 1955, the first prototype turret was sent to Israel and an assembly line to produce it was established there. The first Sherman to be fitted with the new turret was an M4A4, and by 1956 a complete company's worth of the new AFVs had been delivered for combat evaluation.

The new tank was known as the M50 and saw its first action around Abu Agheila, during the 1956 Sinai campaign. Following the campaign various modifications were made and the final version of the M50 Mark I was approved. Production continued and by 1959, a complete battalion's worth of M50s were delivered en bloc to re-equip the 82nd Tank Battalion. At this point it is interesting to note that the Egyptians had also tried to make better use of their old Shermans, even before the Israelis. About 50 M4s were fitted with FL-10 AMX 13 turrets, supplied by another French contractor. The tanks were not a great success and quickly relegated to a secondary role as the Egyptians began to receive more Soviet equipment. Many of the modified Shermans were captured by the IDF and used by them. The M50 did well when it was first introduced, but was clearly not a match for the later Russian T54s and JSIIIs which began to arrive in Egypt in the early 1960s. Even the M50 Mark II, which was based upon the M4A3 and had a Cummins 460 hp diesel engine fitted and HVSS, was still found wanting.

Once again it was the French armament industry that came to the rescue. They had just completed the development of another tank gun – the 105 mm 56-calibre 105F1, a long-barrelled (nearly six metres long), revolutionary weapon, which was designed to fire a specially developed new HEAT round at a muzzle velocity of 1,000 m/sec. Unfortunately the new gun, which the French had designed for their AMX30 main battle tank, was too long and its muzzle velocity too high to operate efficiently in a modified Sherman turret, primarily because there was insufficient space during recoil. The Israeli design team returned to Bourges Arsenal and began work on modifying the new gun to fit Israel's requirements. This resulted in the barrel length being reduced by 1.5 m, bringing the muzzle velocity down to around 800 m/sec. The new gun, now of 44 calibres, was designated as the 105 mm D1504 tank gun. Suitable ammunition, it was agreed, would be made in Israel, thus laying

the foundations of their ammunition manufacturing industry. Of course there was much to be done to the basic Sherman tank, if the rest of the AFV was to match up to the new gun and enable the new tank to stand up to the potential opposition. They decided to start with the basic M4A1 cast hull, not just because they had plenty available, but also because they had been fitted with larger turrets than any other type of Sherman.

First of all, the Cummins 460 hp diesel, as for the M50 Mark II, was fitted plus E8 HVSS suspension, modified steering, transmission, exhaust and wider tracks. The new gun required a new turret mantlet, turret bustle and ammunition stowage, while a light/IR searchlight was fitted over the gun and two smoke dischargers on either side of the turret. The original bulky, cumbersome battery charger was replaced with a compact Laris-Rhône dynamo, while the turret locking assembly and hydraulic controls were replaced by a new system based upon the one fitted in the AMX13. In total these modifications took 2,500 man hours per tank and resulted in an increase of seven tons, bringing the combat weight to 39 tonnes. Despite its high silhouette the tank had a top speed of 28 mph and a range of 170 miles. Finally, during firing trials it was decided to fit a muzzle brake. The M51 was first used in combat prior to the 1967 war, during border conflicts with Syria. Since then it has taken part in many battles, even successfully engaging Soviet T62s in 1973, but is now relegated to reserve brigades and border defence units. They were also used by the Christian Militia in Lebanon.

SELF-PROPELLED ARTILLERY

The first SP artillery to reach the Israelis arrived in late 1956 and comprised some French 105 mm howitzers mounted on AMX13 light tank chassis. They were followed in the 1960s by a variety of other SP guns as the principle of using self-propelled artillery became the 'norm' for IDF. Most of these weapons were based upon the Sherman chassis. For example, following the 1956 Sinai campaign, several batteries of surplus British M7 Priest SPs were obtained, 36 of which were modified in 1962, by the substitution of the French 105 mm howitzer. They were used

Sherman with hydraulically-operated dozer blade for clearing obstacles in forward areas (Christopher Foss (IDF)).

with some success during the Six Day War, but it was clear even then that the old 105 mm howitzer was outdated, having neither the range nor the hitting power to compare with the new Soviet equipments, such as the 122 mm and 152 mm guns which were then being supplied to the Arabs. It was therefore decided to go for a more powerful gun and several French-made M50 155 mm howitzers were mounted on Sherman M4A3 chassis by Israeli Ordnance. In 1968, these SPs were re-engined with the 460 hp diesel engine. Improvements continued and in 1973, the first models of the L33 (M68) 155 mm SP gun came into operational service. Built by the Soltam factory of Haifa, under licence, these were essentially a Sherman M4A3E8 chassis, with a Finnish Tampella 155 mm 33-calibre howitzer mounted in a high-sided casemate, with panoramic as well as direct fire vision equipment, so that the guns could be used in both the direct and indirect fire roles. There were plenty of Sherman chassis available, as they were being phased out and replaced with Centurions and M60s. The L33 has an eight-man gun detachment, including a driver and commander, sitting at the front, with the commander just to the rear and higher than the driver. Both positions have single-piece hatch covers and bullet-proof glass windows to the front and side. The crew have an induction loop internal communications system and the vehicle carries sufficient fuel and ammunition for a typical battlefield day. Sixty rounds are stowed, including 16 ready rounds. The gun has a semi-automatic breech, together with a pneumatic handling and loading system which is recharged from the engine, giving a very high rate of fire.

OTHER MODELS

The inventive Israelis put their old Sherman chassis to various other uses. For example, Soltam also produce a Sherman-based 160 mm SP heavy mortar. The tank has had its turret and superstructure removed and replaced by a vertically-sided armoured box within which the mortar is mounted. In action, the front of the box is folded down to a horizontal position. The breech-loaded mortar can be elevated between 43° and 70°, giving a maximum range of 10,500 yards. 56 mortar bombs are carried plus a crew of eight men. The heavy mortar also mounts a machine-gun for close protection. Latterly it is being replaced by a new model based upon the Centurion which has an all-round traversing turret. There is also an artillery observation vehicle which has had the Sherman turret replaced by a scissors-type hydraulically-operated arm on top of which is

o mm self-propelled
ortar, showing tools
nd equipment and
aside of armoured box.
he vehicle has a crew
eight men and a
aded weight of
,822 lb (Christopher
oss (IDF)).

mounted a platform for use by an OP officer, and is known as the 'Cherrypicker'. The M32 tank recovery vehicle, M4 Crab flail, M4A1 tankdozer and TWABY Sherman bridgelayer have all served with IDF. Finally, there is an armoured ambulance, again with the turret removed, engine moved to the front and the hull used to evacuate wounded from the battle area.

LATIN AMERICA

As one might expect, many Latin American countries have acquired Sherman tanks at one time or another, and many still number them among their active armoured forces. Most of Latin America declared war upon the Axis during World War Two, but only a handful of countries took an active part in the war, apart from providing naval and air base facilities to the Allies. Only the ground troops of one nation – Brazil – served abroad, their 1st Infantry Division being a part of General Mark Clark's US Fifth Army in Italy, where they served with distinction from July 1944 onwards. It has been said that the USA deliberately prevented more Latin American countries from getting involved in the war as they did not want them to gain modern combat experience, but postwar American administrations have supplied many such countries with arms and equipment. The Rio Treaty of Mutual Defence, signed in 1947, gave rise to a number of Latin American countries receiving Sherman tanks among other weapons. Latterly, as the survey below shows, other countries have also supplied Shermans in addition to the USA.

Taking an alphabetical look at the armoured forces of the Latin American countries it can be seen that Argentina has at least 200 Sherman M4s and Sherman Fireflies in their army, which they have obtained from a variety of sources. The Fireflies still form the backbone of their armoured forces, but did not of course take part in the Falklands campaign. Brazil has now relegated the 60 Shermans they acquired from USA in World War Two into reserve, and replaced them with more modern AFVs. The emergence of Brazil as a tank-producing nation in its own right probably means that these Shermans will find other buyers or be put to other uses. For example, Moto Pecas SA have produced a recovery vehicle able to lift ten tons and based upon the Sherman chassis.

They are also designing a 65-foot bridgelayer on the same chassis. Chile was given 30 Shermans by America as a result of signing the Rio Treaty and then purchased a further 46 from commercial sources. Colombia obtained a limited number of M4A3s after World War Two, while Cuba was given seven by the USA in February 1957. Two years later the rebels against whom they had been used had taken over the country and the Shermans! They remained in Cuban Army service and were reputedly used by Castro against the exiled Cubans of 2506 Brigade when they landed in the abortive Bay of Pigs invasion of 16-17 April 1961, so they could well have engaged in tank v tank battles with the invading M41s.

Guatemala obtained ten Shermans from USA after the war and is reported to have them still in service.[31] Mexico obtained 25 Shermans again thanks to the Rio Treaty. Nicaragua has ten M4s, but they were obtained elsewhere, namely from Israel. Nicaragua had been sympathetic to the Israeli cause from the outset and sold the Jews a large quantity of surplus small arms when the State of Israel was established. Their kindness was rewarded some years later, when the Israelis sold President Somoza 45 Staghound armoured cars, some half-tracks and ten Shermans, which they later used against the Sandanista rebels. Paraguay obtained nine Shermans from the USA in 1969, then three Fireflies from Argentina in 1971 and a further three in 1981. Finally, Peru obtained 50 Shermans from the United States at some period after the end of World War Two.

INDO-PAKISTAN WARS

In September 1965, a vicious month-long campaign was fought in the Punjab by India and Pakistan, during which the opposing armoured forces were engaged in some of the largest and most bitter tank battles since the end of World War Two. Sherman tanks were involved on both sides, as well as such derivatives as the M36. Trouble in the area had been simmering ever since India formally annexed Kashmir in 1957, but it was not until 1965 that a full-blooded war broke out between them over the disputed area. In April that year there was fighting in the Rann of Kutch, but a cease-fire was arranged through British mediation on 1 July. However, more serious trouble was brewing as large numbers of Pakistani irregulars began crossing the cease-fire line and entering Indian Kashmir. By 5 August India was claiming that the level of infiltration amounted to a full-scale invasion and they retaliated some three weeks later by sending their own troops over the cease-fire line to capture the guerrilla assembly areas. Pakistan then reacted by launching its own offensive in infantry brigade strength, supported by tanks, in the Chhamb area on 1 September. Five days later the Indians responded, with a three-pronged attack against Lahore, Sialkot and towards Hyderabad in the south. The major armoured battles took place over the next few weeks, but gradually a stalemate developed and the UN Security Council called for a cease-fire, which came into effect on 23 September.

Prior to 1965 both armies had been organised and trained along British lines and were predominantly based on infantry units. However, both had a fair number of tanks. It is difficult to determine accurate figures, but Pakistan appears to have had some 900 main battle tanks, mainly M47 and M48 Pattons and the older Sherman M4. They were faced by some 800 Indian MBTs, mainly Shermans, but with some 300 Centurions. The Pakistanis also had some M36B2 tank destroyers, mounting the 90 mm gun, while both sides had a number of other Sherman variants, such as tank retrievers. The Shermans were mainly of American origin and had been upgraded since the war with HVSS and the 76 mm gun. Undoubtedly the most sophisticated tanks on the battlefield were the Pattons and in theory they should have been able to see off the less sophisticated Centurions and Shermans. The great success of the Centurions in the campaign was mainly due to their much higher level of protection, a factor which has also been proved on many occasions on the battlefields of the Middle East. However, the Indians claim that it was basically the fact that sophisticated equipment was in the hands of unsophisticated soldiers.

To quote from one Indian writer, Lieutenant Colonel (Retd) Dr Bhupinder Singh: '... Tanks themselves were better handled by the Indians, mainly because the Indian tanks were older, simpler and less complicated than the American-made Patton tanks utilised by the Pakistani forces. The sheer modernity of the Patton was its undoing, Indian tanks would fire off three shots while the Pakistanis were twiddling with its computers.'[32] While there is

some truth in what he says, perhaps it is only fair to quote from a book published by the other side which gives a rather different picture: 'That the Patton has proved the better tank is the conversation. It is four miles an hour faster than the Centurion at 24 mph[33] and is more manoeuvrable. The Patton gun is superior they say. The Centurion is too square and bulky, practically any hit causes damage.'[34] In the same way tank casualties were equally differently reported by both sides – Pakistan said they had 161 tanks destroyed and knocked out 475 Indian, while the Indians claimed 471 Pakistani tanks for the loss of only 128 of their own. A more unbiased assessment has put the tank casualties at 250 Pakistan (mainly the older M47 Pattons and Shermans) and the Indians at 80 – 10% of their original total, while the Pakistani figure is some 30%. I doubt if even these figures are really accurate, one main reason being that after the cease-fire, many tanks were able to be recovered from the battlefield by both sides, taken away and repaired, so that they could live to fight another day.

Undoubtedly the Sherman and the M36 proved themselves battleworthy, albeit rather long in the tooth. Battle accounts do not unfortunately often single out the types of individual tanks employed, but this quotation from Colonel Singh's book does contain some references to the Sherman: '62 Cavalry started advancing at 9.30 am ... when it was going round the village of Bhagowal, the Pak Pattons opened fire from the crossroads area. The armour-piercing shots of 62 Cavalry Sherman tanks just ricocheted off the Pattons. They therefore ranged with armour-piercing and fired white phosphorous which successfully knocked out the Pattons ... A large number of Patton tracks were noticed in Bhagowal area after its capture on 13 September ... as 62 Cavalry had only Shermans to fight against Pattons, Colonel B. M. Singh, CO of the Regiment, decided to withdraw by bounds. RHQ was always with the squadron that held the lay back position. The Pak tanks got attracted towards 16 Cavalry which was also deployed next to 62 Cavalry. This split their tank force as they sent the major portion of their armour to engage 16 Cavalry. The only Patton squadron which had been left again 62 Cavalry rushed on to the Indian Shermans in contravention of fire and movement tactics. They learnt a lesson of their life when the

Shermans opened up on them at close range and destroyed three Pattons ... After this battle the superiority and sophistication of the Patton became a thing of the past.'

Following the 1965 war both sides increased their tanks from whatever source they could, the Indians adding the British-designed, Indian-built Vickers Vyjianta and Russian T54/55s while the Pakistanis obtained numerous T59s from China. They were thus both well-equipped in time for the next war in 1971. However, this time the expected armoured battles on the Punjab front did not materialise, mainly because both sides had mined the borders so heavily that armour was unable to move. No doubt a number of Shermans must still have been in service on both sides.

THE FUTURE

The continuing use of the Sherman medium tanks all over the world is well evidenced by the countries covered in this chapter. There are, of course, many others for which information is sketchy: Uganda, for example, was supplied with some Shermans by Israel some years ago, while Yugoslavia is reported to still have some Fireflies and to use both the M32 and M74 TRV. A large number of countries, including Austria, Greece, Japan, Spain and Turkey also have TRVs still in service according to Jane's 'Bible' on armour and artillery. Undoubtedly, the Sherman will continue to be used in one form or another, although it can never be considered a modern battle-winner on a par with current main battle tanks, despite such modernisation as the Israelis have done to its now 40-plus-year-old frame. However, its place in the history of the development of the armoured fighting vehicle is assured.

SHERMAN: A JUDGEMENT

Having described the long and continuing history of this remarkable medium tank, the moment has arrived to endeavour to make a judgement of its overall performance and to decide what special place, if any, it should have in the history of the development of the armoured fighting vehicle. As I explained at the start of this book, the three basic characteristics of a tank are firepower, protection and mobility, success or failure normally depending upon how they are balanced one with the other. On that showing the original Sherman comes out as a very satisfactory but not spectacular gun tank, robust and reliable, but lacking in firepower – for most of its life anyway – while its protection left much to be desired. Purely as a gun tank, therefore, despite the enormous numbers produced, it does not appear to deserve any special accolade.

However, there is another factor to consider which I believe makes all the difference and that is its adaptability. No tank ever before or since the Sherman has been called upon to perform such a wide variety of tasks. The Sherman ideally encompasses those attributes of a weapon which this series, 'Weapons and Warfare', was devised to explore: that a weapon's true measure of success lies in the inherent adaptability of its basic characteristics to new tactical and strategic demands of warfare, and that, devoid of any 'glamour', a tank must first and finally be valued as a weapon system.

Another glance at the photographs in this book will show just how wide ranging has been the jobs given to the Sherman. Man's ingenuity has been allowed to run riot, because the designer has been able to use the basic, robust, reliable Sherman tank on which to hang all the strange, at times bizarre, ideas for overcoming battlefield problems, with the confidence that the Sherman will not let him down. Equally at home as the basis for mounting guns of all calibres, or as a tank destroyer, a self-propelled howitzer a mine clearance vehicle, a rocket carrier, a bridge-layer, a dozer, a recovery vehicle ... the list is endless and ever increasing. Sherman has thus outlived all its contemporaries because of its inherent adaptability and it is this characteristic which has won for the Sherman a unique place in the history of armoured warfare.

This is a series of photographs taken of Judge Jim Osborne's Sherman M4A1E8(76). All the photographs were taken by Bernie Schmitt.

This page and opposite
All round views of the
fully-restored M4A1E

Left. Rear idler wheel.

Far left. Drive sprocke

Horizontal volute spri
suspension.

Drive sprocket.

Rear idler wheel.

'80 23-inch double pin
track.

Dual support roller.

Gun mantlet.

Commander's vision
cupola.

Turret left-hand side.

Loader's escape hatch.

152

ENDNOTES

1. *United States Tanks of World War II,* Blandford Press, 1983.
2. *Desert Rats at War (Europe),* by the author, Ian Allan Ltd.
3. The Ordnance Department: *Planning Munitions for War.*
4. Mr Dewar's Christian name was put on the side of the first Sherman purchased by his Mission. The tank, an M4A1 from Lima Locomotive Works, is preserved at the Tank Museum, Bovington Camp.
5. The Ordnance Department: *Procurement and Supply.*
6. ibid.
7. The crew of the Lee was seven men, commander, 37 mm loader, 37 mm gunner, 75 mm loader, 75 mm gunner, radio operator and driver.
8. TM 9-750 (see bibliography).
9. *An account of the procurement of armoured fighting vehicles in North America by the British Purchasing Commission/British Supply Mission,* written in August 1945.
10. Taken from the Technical Manual for M4 and M4A1 medium tanks, TM 9-731A dated November 1942 (see bibliography).
11. The loader/radio operator was also known as the 'cannoneer'.
12. Later production models of the Sherman also had a small oval hatch for the loader.
13. First production tanks had the Wright R975 EC2 engine fitted; this was later superseded by the R975 C1 Continental engine.
14. The 50 amp, 30 volt auxiliary generator was driven by a two-cycle single-cylinder air-cooled petrol engine.
15. The engine hour meter indicated the total number of hours the engine had been in operation.
16. The M4A2 (Sherman 3) had two clutches, one for each engine, the single clutch pedal operating both clutches simultaneously.
17. Gear ratios were: first, 7.56:1, second, 3.11:1, third, 1.78:1, fourth, 1.11:1, fifth, 0.73:1 and reverse, 5.65:1.
18. 83 for the longer M4A4.
19. Sometimes all this radio equipment provided problems, but a good tanker could always rise to the occasion as this quote from Colonel Oswald C. Costlow, who served in 12th Armored Division, explains:

    'Communication between tanks in a five-tank platoon was primarily via radio. The Platoon Leader and the Platoon Sergeant were authorised one transmitter and one receiver (SCR 528); the other three tanks only had receivers (SCR 538). However, upon reaching Europe we augmented our communications capability by giving the Platoon Leader an extra receiver (SCR 508) so he could listen to both his platoon net and the company net. The three tanks with only one receiver each were given a transmitter then all tanks could both send and receive. Also, because we worked very closely with the Armored Infantry and since our radio and their radio did not net, a Platoon Leader received an Infantry SCR 300, the walkie-talkie radio, that was placed in a small metal basket welded to the side of the turret. In addition to all the radios there was a field telephone tied to the rear right side of the tank and another one inside the turret on top of the radio. This was designed for use in working directly with the Infantryman on the ground. Each had an important purpose and were used whenever necessary.

    'I always knew it would happen and it did! One day my Company Commander radioed; one of my Platoon tanks radioed; the Infantry Platoon Leader, who I was working with, radioed; and yes, someone rang the telephone. What happened? Why, of course, I told my Platoon tank to wait, turned off the Infantry, waved to the telephone caller to wait – and answered my Commander.'
20. Major General Robert W. Grow, Commanding General 6th Armored Division.

21. Quoted in General Bradley's autobiography, *A Soldier's Story*.

22. It was Mr Gibb (later Sir Claude Gibb), a civilian employed at the Ministry of Supply, who, against the advice of higher authority – both technical and military – went ahead and got the gun installed successfully.

23. This estimate was made in May 1942, when it was agreed that the USA and UK would each produce a pilot assault tank – the British one being based upon the Mk VIII Cruiser (Cromwell) and the US one on the M4 Sherman.

24. Taken from a report (1942) on the design and testing of medium M3 tanks as quoted in The Ordnance Department: *Planning Munitions for War*.

25. For a description of the early use of the Satan flame gun in M3A1s at Saipan see Chapter 4 of *United States Tanks of World War II* by the author, Blandford Press, 1983.

26. Lieutenant General Robert C. Richardson, Jr, Commanding General, US Army Forces, Central Pacific Area, as quoted in Final Report COM GEN AF MIDPAC.

27. *The Story of 79th Armoured Division,* published in Hamburg, July 1945.

28. Colonel (later Brigadier General) John K. Christmas, as quoted in The Ordnance Department: *Procurement and Supply.*

29. His memory is incorrect, of course. Maximum thickness of the M4A6 (late production) was only 4.25 to 2.0 inches on the lower front, while sides were 1.5 inches (2 inches on turret sides).

30. Quoted from Office of the Chief of Ordnance document T-1508A, kindly supplied by Richard P. Hunnicutt, Esq.

31. See *Armed Forces of Latin America,* by Adrian J. English.

32. *1965 War (Role of Tanks in India-Pakistan War).*

33. This appears to be slightly adrift. The top speed of a Centurion was about $21\frac{1}{2}$ mph and that of M47 $36\frac{1}{4}$ mph, so it is approximately correct if the comparison is with M47 but not if it is with M48.

34. *Indo-Pakistan War, a flash-back,* published in 1966 by the Department of Films and Publications, Government of Pakistan.

air cleaners Any internal combustion engine requires a constant flow of clean air to function properly. Large, efficient air cleaners are needed for a tank engine as it must be able to cope with dusty, cross-country conditions that would clog any normal engine.

antenna That part of a wireless set which picks up or sends the wireless waves through the ether; also called the aerial. On a tank, the normal working antenna is a flexible, thin rod, mounted in a base on the top of the turret.

appliqué armour An interim method of increasing armour protection, before changes are introduced on the production line, is to add on extra armour, for example by bolting or welding on extra plates, or adding some form of plastic armour. There is a constant battle between firepower and protection, so, as tank and anti-tank guns get more powerful, armour thickness has to be increased in order to survive.

auxiliary generator Used to charge the tank batteries or to provide extra power to run the power traverse and gyrostabiliser, or to heat the turret; it is known affectionately by the Americans as 'Little Joe' and the British as 'Tiny Tim'. On Sherman, it consisted of a 1,500 watt generator, driven by a small, one-cylinder two-stroke, air-cooled petrol engine, complete with its own fuel tank.

ball mount A hemi-spherical mounting for a machine-gun and its sighting gear, allowing, for example, a hull gunner to fire in various directions.

barbette A feature of early American tank design in which additional space was made in the hull by extending the superstructure upwards all round, making the tank into a mobile pillbox, sometimes with a small traversing turret on the top. It was used for additional weapons (usually machine-guns).

bogie The bogies provide support for the weight of the tank and consist normally of a spring suspension unit mounted on an axle and two wheels (known as bogie wheels) which distribute the weight along the track.

bore The inside of the gun barrel.

breech mechanism The mechanical device mounted on the breech ring to close the breech after loading so that it is sealed before firing.

calibre The method of designating the diameter of the bore of a gun, measured in inches, millimetres or centimetres.

chamber That part of the gun into which the round is placed for firing.

chassis The basic part of the tank containing the driver's position, engine and transmission compartments, onto which is mounted the superstructure and turret.

coaxial The mounting of two weapons on the same axis, so that they move together in both elevation and traverse.

cradle That portion of the gun mount which does not recoil.

cupola An armoured dome on top of part of the turret, containing vision devices and incorporating an escape hatch, directly above the tank commander's station.

elevating mechanism The mechanical/other linkage by which the gun is moved vertically around its trunnions.

episcope A method of viewing from a tank, usually comprising a fixed periscope.

face hardened A method of finishing armour so that the outside surface is harder than the rest of the plate.

fighting compartment That part of the tank which contains the main armament and those members of the crew needed to serve it.

firing gear The linkage, mechanical or other, by which the gun is fired.

glacis The armour plate, normally angled, which forms the front and most vulnerable part of the tank chassis.

grouser An extension to the normal track which is added in order to obtain more traction in bad going.

gyrostabiliser A method of maintaining the axis of the gun in the same horizontal and vertical planes, once it has been laid, thus keeping the gun on target even when the tank is moving over rough ground. Early stabilisers would only keep the gun roughly on target.

homogeneous armour A type of armour which has the same chemical and physical characteristics throughout.

idler The undriven wheel mounted at the other end of the chassis to the driving sprocket, it carries the track and can be moved to adjust track tension.

mantlet A large slab of armour in the front of the turret which protects the gun trunnions from enemy fire, normally one of the thickest parts of the tank.

mockup A full size, wooden replica which is built prior to the building of the prototypes.

muzzle brake A specially shaped attachment which is screwed onto the end of the gun barrel and deflects backwards some of the gases following the projectile, in order to reduce recoil.

pilot model The first fully finished model – prior to mass production – normally much of which is hand finished. It will be used to perfect the model before building the prototypes.

pistol port A small opening in the side of the turret, which normally has a plug on a swivel and is used for looking through, ventilation, firing small arms, etc.

popping rivets A phenomenon suffered by riveted armour. When struck by a projectile rivets would burst free of their heads and become projectiles themselves inside the tank.

power-to-weight ratio A way of expressing the potential of a tank, by dividing the weight by the horsepower – normally expressed in brake horsepower (bhp) per ton.

power train The engine, gearbox, drive shafts, final drive, etc, which provides the power to the tracks.

ready rounds Ammunition stowed near to the gun, readily accessible for immediate action.

recoil system The method by which the recoil of the gun is controlled, usually a mixture of springs and buffers. Some of the recoil energy is used to eject the empty case and recock the gun.

recuperator A recoil system which uses compressed air or some other gas instead of a spring.

road wheel The wheels which are in contact with the track and take the sprung weight of the tank.

running gear The suspension of a tank, including the tracks.

sponson An added portion on the side of a tank hull, usually containing a weapon.

sprocket A toothed wheel engaged in the track which is driven by the engine and thus turns the track.

tank An armoured fighting vehicle designed to carry protected firepower about on the battlefield.

tank destroyer An armoured fighting vehicle specifically designed to deal with enemy tanks, so its own protection is sacrificed for maximum firepower and mobility.

top rollers Small rollers mounted at the top of the sides of the chassis on which the tracks run.

track The part which supports and propels the tank across country, it comprises a series of track plates joined together with trackpins.

transmission The method of changing the speed of the drive from the engine to the drive sprockets, the main component being the gearbox.

traverse mechanism The machinery by which the turret is traversed, either manually or electrically.

turret The revolving part of the tank containing the main armament and its crew.

turret ring A toothed ring fastened to the turret which rests on bearings in the turret race which is fixed onto the chassis.

BIBLIOGRAPHY

BOOKS AND MAGAZINES

Anon: *44th Tank Battalion Tank Tracks Tennessee to Tokyo*, published privately.

English, Adrian J.: *Armed Forces of Latin America*, Jane's Publishing Co.

Eshel, Lieutenant Colonel David, and others: *Born in Battle* magazines, Eshel-Dramit Ltd.

Forty, George: *United States Tanks of World War II*, Blandford Press, and *Tanks across the Desert*, William Kimber.

Foss, Christopher F. (editor): *Jane's Armour & Artillery 1984–85*, Jane's Publishing Co.

Gugeler, Russell A.: *Combat actions in Korea*, Office of the Chief of Military History, US Army.

Green, Constance McLaughlin and others: *The Ordnance Department, Planning Munitions for War*, Office of the Chief of Military History, US Army.

Haemmel, William G: *Tank Soldier's Journal*, published privately.

Hofmann, George F.: *The Super Sixth* 6th Armd Div Association.

Hunnicutt, Richard P.: *Sherman, a history of the American Medium Tank*, Presidio Press.

Mayo, Lida and others: *The Ordnance Department on Beachhead and Battlefront*, Office of the Chief of Military History, US Army.

Singh, Lieutenant Colonel (Retd) Dr Bhupinder: *1965 War (Role of Tanks in India-Pakistan War*, BC Publishers.

Stout, Wesley W.: *Tanks are mighty fine things*, Chrysler Corporation.

Thomson, Harry C. and others: *The Ordnance Department, Procurement and Supply*, Office of the Chief of Military History, US Army.

Not known: *The Story of 79th Armoured Division*, published in Hamburg, 1945.

Not known: *Indo-Pakistan War, a flashback*, Department of Films & Publications, Government of Pakistan.

MANUALS

Technical manuals on US military equipment, published by the War Department, Washington as follows:
- TM 9–307 – 75 mm tank guns M2 and M3 plus mounts M1, M34 and M34A1
- TM 9–308 – 76 mm tank guns M1A1C and M1A2
- TM 9–324 – 105 mm howitzer M4
- TM 9–730C – medium tank M3A4
- TM 9–731A, 731AA – medium tanks M4 and M4A1
- TM 9–731B – medium tank M4A2
- TM 9–731G – 3-in GMC M10A1
- TM 9–738 – tank recovery vehicles M32, M32B1, M32B2, M32B3 and M32B4
- TM 9–745 – 90 mm GMC M36B2
- TM 9–748 – 90 mm GMC M36B1
- TM 9–750 – medium tanks M3, M3A1 and M3A2
- TM 9–752 – 3-in GMC M10
- TM 9–753 – medium tank M3A3 and M3A5
- TM 9–754 – medium tank M4A4
- TM 9–756 – medium tank M4A6
- TM 9–759 – medium tank M4A3